COUNTRYSIDE CYCLING IN BEDS, BUCKS AND HERTS.

Mick Payne

D1354096

The
Book
Castle

DEDICATION
To Mum

**First published May 1995
by The Book Castle
12 Church Street, Dunstable, Bedfordshire.**

Monochrome origination by:
Ridgeway Graphics, Daventry, Northants.

Printed by: Antony Rowe Ltd., Chippenham
ISBN 1 871199 92 1

ACKNOWLEDGEMENTS.

Thanks to the following people who have helped ride routes, provided information or just given encouragement.
 My wife Linda, Paul and Joanne Gorton, Rita Howkins, Paul and Gary Short and Emma Munday of Forest Enterprise. Plus of course Paul Bowes of the Book Castle, Dunstable.

CONTENTS

The Rides

Bridleway on Route 2

INTRODUCTION

Although not an area normally associated with mainstream mountain biking, the countryside in Bedfordshire, Buckinghamshire and Hertfordshire can with its many bridleways, steep chalk scarps and open rolling farmland vie with other more glamorous areas. This book aims to give both the local rider and visitor an insight into this underrated area.

Although the rides are aimed mainly at the recreational cyclist (the average length being about 11 miles) the more committed rider will, I hope find something to his/her liking. The routes are circuits using as large a proportion of off-road cycling as is possible, whilst trying to avoid miles of road work.

They may of course often be lengthened, although this will generally result in an imbalance towards road mileage. Route 20 is a combination however, of three shorter routes, and shows, how, by the use of lanes and linking bridleways, a more challenging ride may be constructed. No doubt there will be those who think it the only route in the book worth doing, whilst for lesser mortals it will perhaps remain 'a bit of a challenge'!

All the routes have been ridden by myself, often with my wife or in the company of a few friends, and are all to the best of my knowledge on legal tracks. If any encroach upon a footpath this is mentioned in the text - please dismount and walk. This is a fairly sensitive area used by many members of the public; it would be very easy to bring our sport into disrepute by the action of a few thoughtless individuals.

THE AREA

The area covered by this guide is one of the great recreational locations north of London, bringing with it all the problems of conflicting interests. Walking, horseriding, golf, angling, etc. all have their sometimes fanatical adherents many of whom think of the mountain bike as an invention of Satan himself. Therefore a softly softly approach to riding is probably in order in most places. So hide your tail and horns and get riding.

Geographically the area can be taken as centred on Junction 11 of the M1, between Luton and Dunstable, and includes parts of the counties of Hertfordshire and Buckinghamshire, along with most of Bedfordshire. It takes in much of the eastern end of the Chilterns, as well as the flat lands on the Cambridgeshire border, the Ouse Valley and even canalside locations.

The region is also traversed by the ancient path of the Icknield Way, believed to be the oldest road in Britain, which joins the Peddars Way in Norfolk and the Ridgeway by the Thames at Goring, parts of which are used in routes in this guide. Apart from the interest given by cycling on such an age-old route there is, perhaps because of the importance of the Icknield Way, a wealth of other historically intriguing sites in the area. I have tried to give details of any interesting places either in or just after the route description.

LOCATION MAP

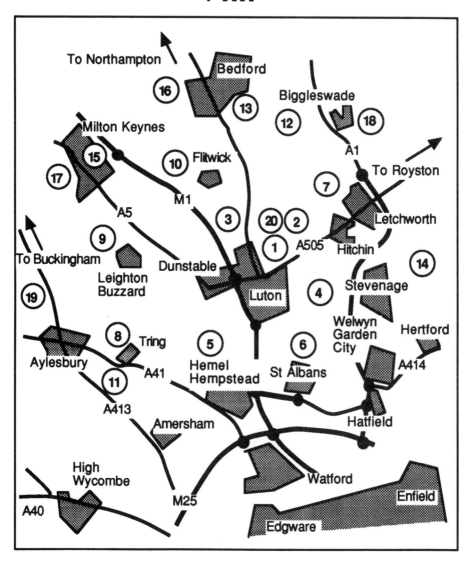

YOUR BICYCLE

The aim of this book is not to try to tell you what type of bike you should use nor how to maintain it. There are plenty of books on the market which do that better than I could; however I think a few words are still appropriate.

The most important thing is that your bicycle is always safe and reliable, and that you know the possible limitations of your particular machine. Generally the cheaper the bike the less abuse it will take, although it is certainly not necessary to arm yourself with a £2000 "superbike" to ride any of the routes in this book. Whenever possible clean and maintain your own bike paying particular attention to the chain, brakes and tyres. Frequent washing is one of the best ways of keeping an eye on the mechanical condition of various components and will often highlight a problem before something breaks.

As far as maintenance is concerned the tools which come with a new bicycle are of severely limited use, and it is worth building up a set of good quality tools for home use as well as a small tool kit to carry with you. The actual tools you collect will depend upon the requirements of your particular bike, and those which I have found useful are listed below.

The first four items I would consider essential, as it is generally preferable to change an inner tube rather than try to repair a puncture, although it may well come to that in the event of another flat. Whilst researching one of the routes for this book I suffered three in quick succession!

For Carrying on Rides:

A - spare inner tube,
B - puncture repair kit, including a spare valve and a short length of old inner tube,
C - 2 tyre levers,
D - tyre pump or possibly a couple of CO_2 cartridges and an adaptor,
E - spoke key, there is a difference in nipple size between European built and Far Eastern wheels,
F - 8, 9 and 10mm socket spanner,
G - 4, 5 and 6mm Allen keys,
H - small adjustable spanner with a short length of duct tape (a very sticky cloth backed tape) wrapped around the handle,
J - headset and pedal spanner,
K - chain link extractor/rivet tool,
L - rear inner brake cable, if used on the front the excess can be wound up and taped out of harms way,
M - small bottle of oil suitable for lubricating chain.

Extra Tools or Spares to Use at Home or Carry as Necessary:

N - spanner or socket for crank nuts/bolts, and a spare nut or bolt,
O - freewheel removing tool of the relevant type,
P - crank removing tool,
Q - pliers capable of cutting control cables,
R - small screwdriver,
S - pair of cone spanners,
T - oil and a small tin or tube of grease,
U - another spare inner tube and spare brake blocks.

I personally do not bother to take a screwdriver on rides as I always carry a Swiss Army Knife, which I have so far found adequate, also if taking bicycles away for any length of time I would pack my workstand. This a small folding one that supports the rear stays thereby holding the wheel clear of the ground and is especially useful for gear adjustments.

Remember also that lights and reflectors are required by law after dark. Even if you do not ride after dark it is a good idea if your bike has the type of reflectors mounted off the fork crown and bridge above the rear tyre to leave them on, as in the event of a brake cable snapping they will stop the straddle wire dropping onto the tyre.

Also with regard to lights, if you transport your bike by car on a rear mounted rack it is illegal to obscure either the rear lights or the number plate. So to conform with the Road Vehicles Lighting Regulations and the Road Traffic Act it is necessary to fit a fully functioning trailer board wired into the car's electrics. In the absence of a trailer board it may be possible to remove the bicycle's wheels and position it so that it does not interfere with lights or number plate.

So stay safe and have fun.

PERSONAL SAFETY

Cycling off-road in this area does not have many of the risks associated with mountainous areas but a few basic safety items are a good idea.

A HELMET is probably the most important buy after your bicycle. Try as many as you can and purchase one which fits well and is comfortable, and conforms to ANSI Z90.4 and SNELL B84 standards.

GLOVES are an item ignored by many but a good pair of padded cycling gloves can protect your hands in the event of a fall and are useful for absorbing some of the shock transmitted from the terrain. I once read that to cycle more than about five miles without gloves is to risk damage to the nerves of the hand. I prefer not to chance it.

FOOTWEAR is a personal choice, but there is no doubt that proper cycling shoes or boots, with their more rigid sole construction are worthwhile. Most people will of course opt to wear trainers of some sort, although the combination of toe-clips and winter mud will soon reduce these to shadows of their former selves. I do also find a bit of ankle support advantageous when having to throw out a steadying foot.

CLOTHING is again a very personal thing but whatever you wear it is best to follow the principle of layering. A number of thin layers allows more control of insulation than one thick one. In the summer I will wear a top made from one of the modern sweat wicking fabrics and padded cycling shorts, which I can supplement with a fleece, windproof top and tracksuit bottoms when the weather gets colder.

It is of course wise to carry some sort of waterproof at any time of the year. There are plenty of cycling dedicated waterproofs in modern breathable fabrics on the market, although I have found a walking type jacket perfectly adequate, perhaps mainly because I already have one!

A FIRST AID KIT including an assortment of plasters, some antiseptic wipes, a small roll of tape and perhaps a bandage are worth carrying for the inevitable cuts and grazes. I carry a small mountaineering kit which is quite comprehensive but compact. These can be bought from most outdoor type shops.

FOOD AND DRINK cannot be ignored as off-road cycling consumes calories at an enormous rate. It is therefore wise to carry some food containing the type of sugars the body can benefit from; bananas are of course very good, as are many of the cereal type bars now obtainable. Chocolate although easy to carry and very palatable is less suitable and is inclined to give an energy 'high' followed by a corresponding low.

Fluid loss can also be a problem so it is essential to replace it by having plenty to drink both before and during the ride. I find the isotonic drinks now on sale very satisfactory, but this may just be psychological.

LUGGAGE of some description is going to be necessary, if only to carry tools and spares. I have found the best combination to be that of a small under seat pack to carry all the items necessary for the wellbeing of the machine, plus a rucksack for my own fuel and clothing. Panniers, racks and the like, although the best option on roads, tend to snag in the undergrowth too easily.

MAPS AND ACCESS

The sketch maps in this book are drawn using my own experience of the terrain, and I have tried to indicate the type of going to be expected. They are not all drawn to the same scale and are not meant to be used without an OS map. Details of relevant maps are given at the start of each route description. Ordnance Survey Landranger Series 1:50 000 sheets 152, 153, 165 and 166 cover all the routes in this book.

A six figure map reference is given for the start of each route and for any particular places of interest which may be nearby. Most of the routes can be added to, ridden in the opposite direction or started and finished in different places. A good map will aid you in these decisions, although I hope you will enjoy the routes as they are.

Judging from the number of bicycles I now see on the back and roofs of cars, I have assumed that many people will be using vehicles to reach the start of the rides so have given wherever possible information on parking. Please remember that some of the parking is in residential areas so be discreet.

The distances given in the route introduction are cumulative from the recommended start point and I have also given a rough estimation of the time necessary for each route. These are based on my own findings, so should easily be shortened by anyone remotely fit or skilful. The times do not allow for stops for punctures, photos, pubs or calls of nature; if you are in the habit of stopping frequently for food and drink or fall off a lot then the times will need adjusting accordingly.

Although primarily a mountain bike guide most of the routes can be ridden on any type of bicycle with perhaps a little more walking or risk of damage to the machine. The rides taking in the Icknield Way or canal tow paths are probably most suitable, and can be modified to miss out the bumpiest/ wettest/ steepest bits to suit.

I have tried also at the end of each route to give an indication of places of interest near-by and any bike shops in the vicinity which may be of help to a visitor (these infer no recommendation, and are for reference only).

Please Remember only ride where you have a legal right to do so, if in any doubt regarding the status of a path or track dismount and walk, and follow the recommendations in the Off Road and Country Codes.

THE OFF ROAD CODE - Issued by the Mountain Bike Club.

- Only ride where you know you have a legal right.
- Always yield to horses and pedestrians.
- Avoid animals and crops. In some circumstances this may not be possible, at which times contact should be kept to a minimum.
- Take all litter with you.
- Leave all gates as found.
- Keep the noise down.
- Don't get annoyed with anyone; it never solves any problems.
- Always try to be self sufficient, for you and your bike.
- Never create a fire hazard.

THE COUNTRY CODE - Issued by the Countryside Commission.

- Enjoy the countryside and respect its life and work.
- Guard against risk of fire.
- Fasten all gates.
- Keep your dogs under close control.
- Keep to public paths across farmland.
- Use gates and stiles to cross fences, hedges and walls.
- Leave livestock, crops and machinery alone.
- Take your litter home.
- Help keep all water clean.
- Protect wildlife, plants and trees.
- Take special care on country roads.
- Make no unnecessary noise.

PUBLIC RIGHTS OF WAY

It is an important part of your off-road cycling to know where you may or may not ride. The following information is intended to help when modifying routes in this book or for planning routes of your own.

A Public Right of Way means only that a right to pass over otherwise private land has been granted, in most cases established by usage or in others as a concessionary right granted by the landowner. This area has one of the oldest tracks in the country in the form of the Icknield Way, which indeed is used in some of the rides in this book.

Please remember that to many users of countryside paths a fast moving mountain bike is the equivalent of a car, and is often perceived as a dangerous vehicle. So always try to be considerate to other people, I have invariably found that slowing down and just saying "hello" tends to get a favourable response.

PUBLIC FOOTPATHS have right of way on foot only. Cyclists have **no** right to ride on them, and the continued abuse by some members of the mountain bike riding community serves only to antagonise the legal users. Landowners are allowed to sue for trespass anyone in breach of this. Footpaths are normally clearly marked as such or may be denoted by a boot symbol or a yellow disc or arrow, and are denoted by short red dashes on OS Landranger Maps.

PUBLIC BRIDLEWAYS have right of way on foot, horseback and pedal cycle although cyclists must give way to walkers and horseriders. Access to pedal cycles was granted in 1968 by Section 30 of the countryside Act. The area does have a large number of riding schools and individuals riding horses so giving way is even more relevant than in some other areas. I have always taken the attitude that the horses were there first, so invariably stop to let them pass. Besides which they are much bigger than me! Bridleways are generally marked similarly to footpaths but with a horseshoe symbol or blue disc or arrow, and appear on OS maps as long red dashes.

BYWAYS/BOATS are open to all traffic, although any vehicles using them must be road legal. They may be marked by finger posts or signs identified by a red disc or arrow. BOATS appear on OS maps as a short red dash followed by a plus sign.

RUPPS or roads used as public paths normally have the minimum status of a bridleway, although many have full vehicular rights. They are in the process of being reclassified as one of the above, and are denoted by a short red dash followed by a longer one on OS maps.

UNCLASSIFIED ROADS are normally shown white on 1:50 000 series OS maps, and may or may not be surfaced. They normally have the same status as a byway or BOAT although many are private and some carry only footpath or bridleway rights.

CYCLE TRACKS are rarely found in this area although the nearby city of Milton Keynes has its own system of "Redways", which are purpose designed tracks, many in parkland, crisscrossing the city. A useful guide may be obtained from the Milton Keynes Borough Council showing all the routes and the type of countryside they cover. I have included one such route, which I hope will provide a good alternative if the other routes may be out of condition or you just don't feel like cleaning the bike yet again.

Another traffic free cycling alternative exists to the south and east of Bedford in the form of the old Bedford-Sandy railway. It is possible at present to cycle from Kempston to the Gt Barford road, although it is envisaged that by 1997/8 the route will go all the way to Sandy. The Willington to Priory Park section has been used in one of the routes in this book.

CANAL TOW PATHS can come under the control of either local councils or British Waterways, and except for those within the "Redway" system used to require a permit. This is no longer necessary, although at the time of writing (1994) it is necessary to obtain a letter of consent, obtainable from British Waterways. Before venturing onto a towpath it is probably worth checking with British Waterways.

Tow paths have a unique problem for cyclists, namely anglers! During the coarse fishing season it may be necessary to keep stopping every few yards, so routes using tow paths are probably best ridden between March and mid June or during the winter months.

MAPS

It is a good idea to supplement the sketch maps in this guide with good large scale maps. The Ordnance Survey Landranger Series are of course the ideal choice and the relevant sheet numbers are given in the introduction to each route.

Changes do occur however so if in any doubt about a right of way it is best to consult the definitive map for the applicable area. These can be found at the offices of all County Councils where they may be freely viewed.

Whilst every care has been taken in the compilation of the routes in this book to follow legal rights of way changes may have taken place or mistakes made. So if challenged by a landowner or farmer who thinks you are trespassing remain calm and polite and leave their land by the shortest acceptable route. If you think you were in the right it is worth checking the definitive maps, and if necessary bring the problem to the attention of the correct authority who should be able to deal with it. The author would also be grateful for notification c/o the publisher. Above all try to avoid confrontations. They do mountain biking no favours at all.

ROUTE RECKONER

I have avoided giving grades for routes, as what one person may find difficult, another will think easy. Also the conditions pertaining at the time make quite a difference to one's perception of a ride. Instead, the next few pages contain a chart giving some idea of what is likely to be met. This may be used as a short cut for finding a suitable outing, or just as a means of disagreement!

It is arranged in columns relating to each particular route. The mileage is that which I have found using the cycle computer on my own bicycle, so the chances of anyone agreeing with that are very slim indeed. The percentage of 'off-road' speaks for itself, although what constitutes 'off-road' is probably less clear. My interpretation is that of any cycling on a legal track, including cycle tracks and Redways.

I have graded the last three columns with stars. In the case of 'Hills', the following apply, *** either no up-hills at all or only slight, ** moderate hills, * steep hills. There is also an 'r' against some one star routes, this indicates that the hill although steep is on road, much easier! Of course none of the routes in this book have really sustained or steep hills, so if you have been training for a place on the Tour de France, you probably won't even notice them!

'Winter' is probably more important, and here a one star route implies that it will be MUDDY, if not all over, then enough to make cycling unpleasant and also to risk damage to the surface of the track. ** are probably normal, some mud, but generally ridable in almost any conditions, and *** routes are on well surfaced bridleways or purpose made cycle routes.

A Root Strewn Uphill

The 'Children' column is perhaps the most contentious, for the youngsters themselves at least. I have included it to give some idea as to whether the routes are suitable for those bicycles having wheels smaller than the normal 26 inches of adult cycles. These bikes also usually suffer in the gear department, and the younger children may not have the stamina for some of the longer up-hills, nor the technical ability for perhaps fast and bumpy down-hills. But don't tell them I said so!

Here the stars are one for the least suitable, up to three for those that can be attempted by children of almost any age. I have also added provisos to the stars in the form of an 's', which is to mean summer, ie a route that although not unsuitable for a 21 speed large wheeled machine in winter may be hard work on a smaller bike. The other is 'c', this means that the route runs alongside a canal, where a moment's inattention could result in a soaking or perhaps even worse.

I hope that the sketch maps provided for each route fill in the gaps, and allow a full assessment to be made, they may also prove useful to those attempting the routes on skinny tyred bikes. Basically the more stars, the easier the route. But don't forget the mileage!

ROUTE NUMBER	LENGTH	% 'OFF-ROAD'
1	6 miles	88 %
2	11 miles	91 %
3	10.1 miles	41 %
4	7.6 miles	42 %
5	7.6 miles	68 %
6	10 miles	55 %
7	9.5 miles	70 %
8	17.4 miles	65 %
9	10 miles	58 %
10	15.2 miles	57 %
11	12 miles	45 %
12	9.5 miles	66 %
13	8.5 miles	75 %
14	10.4 miles	54 %
15	12 miles	100 %
16	9.5 miles	71 %
17	9.2 miles	76 %
18	8.8 miles	72 %
19	15.6 miles	51 %
20	23.6 miles	72 %

HILLS	WINTER	CHILDREN

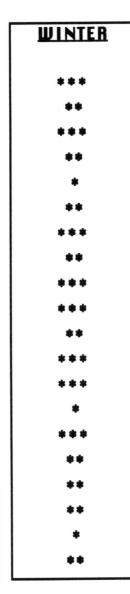

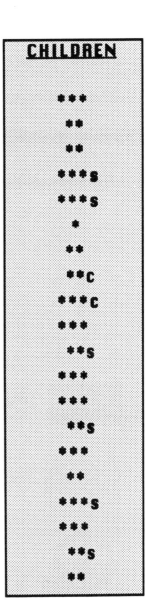

KEY TO MAPS

———————— MAJOR ROADS

———————— MINOR ROADS

———————— WELL DRAINED, OFTEN
SURFACED BRIDLEWAYS

 UNSURFACED, OFTEN
MUDDY BRIDLEWAYS

———————— FOOTPATHS

 RIVERS/CANALS

 POWER LINES

 BUILDINGS

ENCLOSED
GARDENS

 WOODS

LAKES

 UP-HILL

DOWN HILL

Icknield Way

HISTORICAL SITE
OR TRACK

1. WARDEN HILL RIDGE.

DISTANCE:	6 miles/9.6 km (0.7 miles/1.1 km on roads).
HEIGHT GAIN:	197 ft/60 m.
TIME:	1 to 1.5 hours.
MAP:	OS 1:50 000 Sht 166.
CHILDREN:	Very Suitable.
WINTER:	Very Suitable.
START:	OS 086259.

This compact route is ideal for a summer evening or a short daytime ride, and is easily linked with route 2 to give an appreciably longer trip. It is also mostly on well surfaced tracks so can be ridden in just about any conditions. The start point in Links Way (OS 086259) has adequate parking and a board giving information about Warden Hills, from which the route begins.

Set off in a rightwards direction parallel to the main ridge of Warden Hills. Follow a good path across flat grassland until after passing a new housing development it becomes a wider farm track. After 1 mile a crossing is reached and our bridleway takes a left hand turn up a stony track leading towards the ridge, there are concrete blocks here to prevent access to cars. Starting level it gets steeper as it goes, and the steepest part is dissected by large erosion channels. I once stared at these so hard riding up that my front wheel was drawn towards one as if by a magnet and I fell off. I can handle falling off downhill, but uphill !

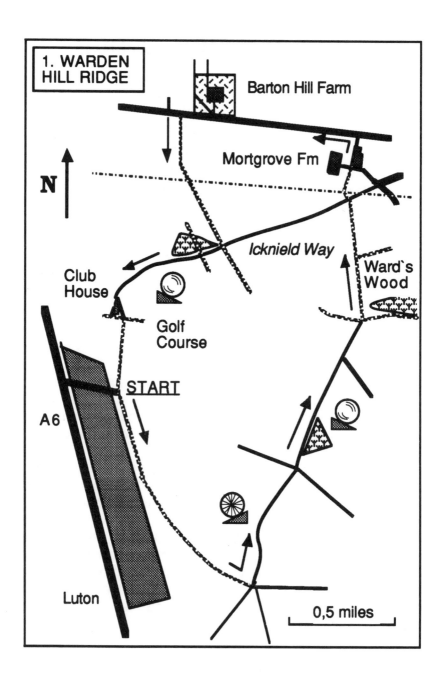

1. WARDEN HILL RIDGE

Barton Hill Farm

Mortgrove Fm

N

Icknield Way

Club House

Ward`s Wood

Golf Course

START

A6

Luton

0,5 miles

Having avoided the ruts the ridge is soon reached, and being a bridleway makes a good way to link this route with the Telegraph Hill one; however our way on this occasion goes straight over and down the other side. The descent is on a good stony surface which coupled with excellent visibility can, if clear, allow an exhilarating run.

At the foot of the hill the same direction is maintained, crossing a wide grassy track by Ward's Wood (2.2 miles). This is followed over a slight rise until the ancient Icknield Way is crossed and a further bridleway leads to Mortgrove Farm where at 3.2 miles a road is reached.

Turn left onto the road and look out for the next bridleway sign on the left, at 3.9 miles just past Barton Hills Farm. Take this track passing under the power lines back to the Icknield Way where a right turn leads past an information board amongst the trees. The now excellent track is followed downhill past the golf course to its club house where either the club access road or a parallel bridleway leads back to the start.

Start point of Route 2

Local bike shops -   Bloomfield Cycles
                        21 Bloomfield Avenue
                        Luton
                        Tel. (01582) 454477

                        Chainey's Cycles
                        28 Chapel Street
                        Luton
                        Tel. (01582) 24436

                        Dyson's Cycle Shop
                        117 Biscot Road
                        Luton
                        Tel. (01582) 33450

                        Levitt's
                        288 Dunstable Road
                        Luton
                        Tel. (01582) 27511

Places of Interest -   Luton's 14th century Parish
                        Church, the largest in
                        Bedfordshire.

                        Luton Museum and Art
                        Gallery in Wardown Park
                        houses displays about
                        local straw hat making and
                        the industrial development
                        of the town.

2. TELEGRAPH HILL

DISTANCE:	11 miles/17.6 km (1 mile/1.6 km on roads)
HEIGHT GAIN:	426 ft/130 m.
TIME:	2.5 hours.
MAP:	OS 1:50 000 Sht 166
CHILDREN:	Fairly Suitable.
WINTER:	Fairly Suitable.
START:	OS 109283

Starting from the Treasures Grove car park at the foot of Telegraph Hill, where there is an information board giving details about the area (OS 109283) this route can be ridden as described or combined with route No. 1 to give a longer ride. It can also be easily shortened by following one of the many bridleways in this area. Unfortunately one of the tracks can be very muddy, indeed after one particularly wet period it took us about six hours to complete. Our frames have good mud clearance but still clogged up enough to prevent the wheels turning. You have been warned !

After lifting your bike over the bridle gate set off in a north-easterly direction up the hill, and follow the rutted green track to a parting of the ways at 0.6 miles. Take the Icknield Way track along the edge of a wood to Telegraph Hill. Named after the telegraph station built here in 1808 to link the Admiralty in London to Great Yarmouth, there are also the remains of a Bronze Age tumulus dating from 2000-1500 BC. On top of the hill it is best to take paths over to the right before starting downhill to the B655 which is reached after 2 miles.

At the road turn right, care is needed here and follow it towards Hitchin until after a few hundred yards a gravel farm track leads off rightwards. Take this rather potholed way and follow it through the grounds of Wellbury House until after a sharp uphill section a cottage is reached (3.4 miles). Go to the right of the cottage, cross the road going to Little Offley and follow the bridleway straight ahead. In wet conditions this track can be very muddy, but if it is then there is probably worse to come!

Although sticky at first, a broad grassy thoroughfare is soon reached which gives pleasant riding until at 4.3 miles at a crossing of bridleways a right turn is made. Now going uphill, again alongside a field, a wood is soon reached. Once under the trees the path is frequently very boggy in places, so it may be a good idea to push around the worst parts to minimise any damage. Compensation is however on hand in the form of small fallen saplings which often lay across the firmer sections, and can give good bunny hop practice. Re-emerging into daylight a line of pylons are the next goal and are about 5.2 miles from the start.

Immediately beneath the cables a bridleway leads almost back the way we have come towards the edge of a wood, where a path marked on the map as a RUPP leads off rightwards down the hill. After passing through a narrow neck of wood this gives a fairly steep descent to the road below (6 miles), where a left turn is made. This leads directly to the village church and a turning on the right which is taken (if you have greater will power than I) past The Lilley Arms which has an excellent garden, serves good food and real ale. Having supped of Abbot Ale or Isostar the road is followed to its end where it curves round and deteriorates rapidly. I don't think that even in the hottest summer this track dries out totally; in really wet weather it can be a nightmare.

At the end of the narrow section the way widens and gains a gravel surface as it runs around the edge of Ward's Wood (see route 1) only to become grassy again as it runs slightly downhill. At 8 miles a gravelly track to the left is taken which climbs gradually

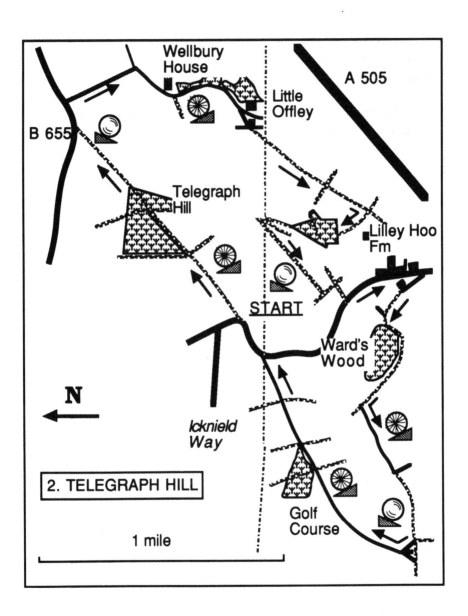

Wellbury House

A 505

B 655

Little Offley

Telegraph Hill

Lilley Hoo Fm

START

Ward's Wood

N

Icknield Way

2. TELEGRAPH HILL

Golf Course

1 mile

until at a 90 degree bend another bridleway carries straight on. This is followed between Warden and Galley Hills and passes Dray's Ditches, an Iron Age defensive dyke. The other side of the hill is the golf course and the Icknield Way which is rejoined at 9 miles.

Turning right onto the Way it is just a couple of miles of easy cycling along it, with the last short stretch on a minor road back to the start point.

Local bike shops -   See Route 1

Places of Interest -   Barton Hills and
                       Ravensburgh Castle,
                       an Iron Age hill fort
                       of 22 acres.

                       Sharpenhoe Clappers
                       with its crown of
                       beeches is one of the
                       most dramatic
                       outcrops of The
                       Chilterns in this area.

                       Sundon Hills
                       Country Park is a Site of
                       Special Scientific
                       Interest and is listed
                       as an Area of Outstanding
                       Natural Beauty.

3. SHARPENHOE AND BARTON

DISTANCE:	10.1 miles/16.2 km (6 miles/9.6 km on roads).
HEIGHT GAIN:	394 ft/120 m.
TIME:	2 hours.
MAP:	OS 1:50 000 Sht 166
CHILDREN:	Fairly Suitable.
WINTER:	Very Suitable.
START:	OS 065296

Although this route has comparatively little 'off-road' mileage, it is still not to be taken too lightly, as the climb from Barton to the top of the hills is fierce and steep. The surfaces are generally good, and it is a fine bad weather route. There is ample parking at the start, at the Sharpenhoe Clappers car park (OS 065296), where there is also an information board.

From the car park, the first bit is easy in the extreme, it swoops down the steep road to a house called Moleskin, where on the left a well surfaced bridleway leads off. As you carry your bike over the bridle-gate it is worth taking a look back at the steep scarp of the Clappers, and perhaps imagine what life would have been like for the occupants of the Iron Age hill fort on its very top.

The next mile or so is superb, as the sandy track meanders along the bottom of the hills, soon turning sharply down, then left to cross a small brook. Just after this, at 1.4 miles, a pair of ponds are passed, the one on the left being full of small rudd, which may often be seen on the surface. Ride between these and continue to the surfaced lane (1.7 miles) where a right turn is made.

Continue pleasantly along the lane, until at 2.8 miles a right turn is made onto a larger road. Just round a bend, it is possible to take a bridleway on the left to a small wood, this then leads back to the road opposite the Linmore Arms. This does not give particularly pleasant cycling, so unless you are desperate to add a few more off-road miles is probably best avoided.

The small pond

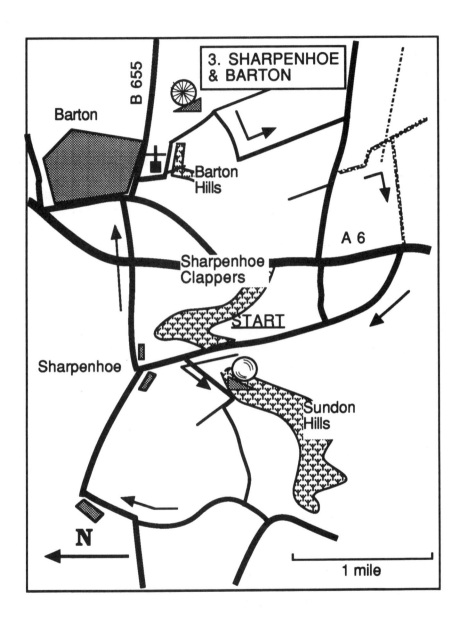

3. SHARPENHOE & BARTON

Barton

B 655

Barton Hills

Sharpenhoe Clappers

A 6

START

Sharpenhoe

Sundon Hills

N

1 mile

At 5.3 miles Barton is reached at the Royal Oak pub, cross the main A6 and take the small road leading off to the left. Continue bearing left, until in a further 0.4 miles a no-through road leads off to the church. This soon becomes a gravel track, and a bridleway is found on the left. Sandy at first, it soon leads to the entrance to the Barton Hills Nature Reserve (6 miles).

As the only access to the reserve is on foot we must continue along the now grassy track alongside. The price of that exhilarating downhill at the beginning now has to be paid. The track becomes flinty and loose, and rears steeply up to the skyline, climbing about 200 ft in just a few hundred yards. Fortunately it soon levels out to contour the beautiful incut hills of the reserve, and at 6.7 miles turns right to descend slightly to a good track where a left turn is made.

This is followed easily (it has sometime in the past been surfaced) to the road (7.5 miles). Turn right, and cycle slightly uphill for a few hundred yards to a bridleway starting amongst a clump of bushes, the sign is almost hidden, and turn left. Follow this alongside a field first left, then right, until directly beneath the pylons.

8.1 miles, and turn right down the rutted track, more or less beneath the pylons all the way to the quaintly named Swedish Cottages. Here at 8.9 miles the road is reached, cross over to take the lane immediately opposite, towards Streatley. The road curves round, and passes a virtually dried up pond, the church and the Chequers pub, to meet a tee-junction at 9.4 miles where a right turn is made. From here it is just a short distance back to the car park.

Local Bike Shops-   See Route 1.

Places of Interest-   See route 2.

4. WHITWELL AND St. PAUL'S WALDEN

DISTANCE:	7.6 miles/12.1 km (4.4 miles/7 km on roads).
HEIGHT GAIN:	338 ft/103 m.
TIME:	2 hours.
MAP:	OS 1:50 000 Sht 166
CHILDREN:	Very Suitable unless Flooded.
WINTER:	Very Suitable.
START:	OS 176219

This short figure of eight route is ideal for a summer evening or perhaps a short daytime ride, and is especially suitable for those with children, as it can be combined with a visit to the Water Hall Farm. If taking children it is best to wait for dry conditions, as the ford will then be shallower, and there is less risk of the riverside section being flooded. Parking is available in a lay-by opposite the Five Wells Cress Farm (OS 176219).

Leave the lay-by, and cycle down the road away from Whitwell. At 0.5 miles a RUPP is reached on the left. The fun begins! The way drops slightly, straight to the ford, this is crossed (if the water is deep expect wet feet!) and the track curves rightwards to run briefly alongside the river. This stretch can be very wet if the river has recently been over its banks, and may prove worse than the actual crossing. Good for photos of struggling companions though!

After pausing to empty your shoes, follow the well surfaced track uphill alongside a hedge to the road. Turn right and follow the road around bends to a footpath sign pointing left (0.9 miles). Ignore this of course, but take the gravel track leading away from the road. After a short distance, where the track peels off leftwards another RUPP leads enticingly across fields.

The next mile or so provides excellent off-road cycling, as the well surfaced, well defined track leads first past a farm, then across fields towards The Holt Farm. The going varies between gravel tracks and narrow, grassy paths as it descends and then climbs from a prominent dip. At 2.1 miles the road is reached at a cluster of remote buildings, turn left towards the prominent water tower.

At the tee junction turn left on to the B 651, and continue to the water tower. A byway descends from the tower fairly steeply through a canopy of trees. It is narrow, bumpy and in places very stony, which combined with the lack of forward visibility demands care. It soon however opens out, and the houses of Whitwell are visible to the right just before a road is reached.

Turn right (3 miles) and coast downhill into the village and turn right again. The road, already narrow, is often made worse by the presence of parked cars, so care is again in order as the poor cyclist is forced out into the centre of the road. Soon however, at 4 miles a road on the left may be taken, which leads past the Water Hall Farm Centre and the Higgletea Piggletea Tea Rooms where a sign declares that cyclists are particularly welcome. Miss the tea and cakes? No chance!

Full of tea and buns the next bit is not going to be easy, a sharp, but thankfully short uphill to the village of St Paul's Walden. Opposite the Strathmore Arms (4.8 miles) turn right, signposted to Easthall and Langley, and cycle pleasantly along lanes to Easthall

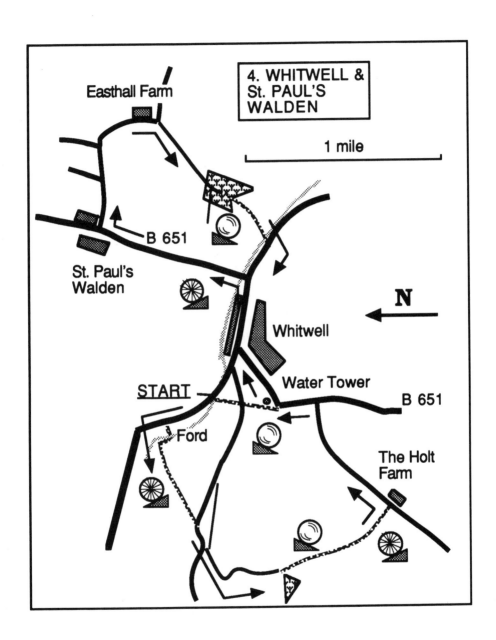

4. WHITWELL &
St. PAUL'S
WALDEN

1 mile

Easthall Farm

B 651

St. Paul's
Walden

Whitwell

N

Water Tower

START

B 651

Ford

The Holt
Farm

Farm. On a bend just after the duck pond a byway sign marks the start of the next stretch of 'off-road'.

At first, broad gravelly going, the route soon becomes narrower along the edge of a wood where it narrows and steepens considerably. The going becomes quite demanding as it traverses tree roots and picks a way through the flints before again opening out and crossing the river again just before the road (6.8 miles). All that remains now is to negotiate Whitwell village again and return to the start via the road.

Local Bike Shops-   Custom Riders
                     55 Bancroft
                     Hitchin
                     Tel. (01462) 437035

                     Frost & Son
                     94 Walsworth Road
                     Hitchin
                     Tel. (01462) 434433

Places of Interest- St. Paul's Waldenbury is the
                     home of the Bowes Lyon family,
                     and where the Queen Mother
                     spent part of her childhood. The
                     gardens are sometimes open to
                     the public.

                     Hitchin is an interesting town
                     with a twice weekly open
                     market. It also boasts an
                     impressive old church.

5. WATER END AND GADDESDEN ROW.

DISTANCE:	7.6 miles/12.2 km (2.4 miles /3.8 km on roads).
HEIGHT GAIN:	223 ft/ 68 m.
TIME:	1.5 to 2 hours.
MAP:	OS 1:50 000 Sht 166
CHILDREN:	Very Suitable in Summer.
WINTER:	Fairly Suitable.
START:	OS 039103

This route is eminently suitable for those with children, or anyone perhaps still not sure of themselves 'off-road'. Although it starts with a fair amount of road work, it does at least mean that the steep uphill is performed on tarmac, which means that the ride finishes with a good downhill. There is also no really technical riding to contend with.

Start from the National Trust car park at Water End (OS 039103) and turn carefully right onto the A 4146, just opposite the Red Lion pub turn left and almost immediately begin climbing. Ascend zig-zags, passing Gaddesden Place and the Crown and Sceptre at Briden's Camp until the road begins to level out.

It soon becomes a pleasant ride along an archetypal English country lane as it undulates between tree-clad banks to Gaddesden

Row (2.2 miles). Go briefly left, and almost immediately right, signposted to Markyate, follow this road until at 2.4 miles a bridleway is found just beyond a wood. The cycling is now almost completely off-road!

Follow the track, which is restrained by a fence, alongside the wood. This, like many riders' routes when fenced can be very muddy. Pass Upper Wood Farm at a footpath and continue in the same direction, still fenced, to a muddy depression by a tree. Here the way enters a wood, and the track winds narrowly through the undergrowth.

We soon emerge to another fenced section, this time with the trees on the left, until a gap in an old iron fence is taken, often muddily! A short distance into this section, a series of small trees lie across the track (mountain bike traps?), which can be very slippery to cross if at all wet.

Becoming broader again, the way leads down towards a farm, and turns first right, then left to emerge onto the road (3.4 miles). This is taken leftwards, to a fairly sharp bend at 3.75 miles and a bridleway sign pointing diagonally right.

Lift your bike over the bridlegate and take the well surfaced track as it undulates across the landscape. A wood is soon reached, and typical of many of them in this area the drainage is rather poor. If you do this in winter, one section of the track almost resembles a pond!

At 4.2 miles Holtsmere End is reached where a bridleway leads off rightwards, signposted Water End Road. Although this can be muddy in places, it is generally broad enough to find a dry line for your wheels. After about half a mile the going becomes surfaced again as it winds superbly downhill, before curving to the right to climb again. As the power lines are approached care is needed, as

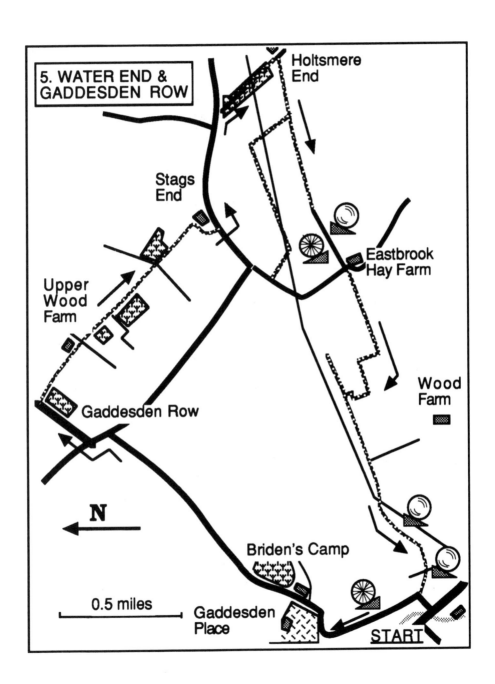

5. WATER END &
GADDESDEN ROW

Holtsmere
End

Stags
End

Eastbrook
Hay Farm

Upper
Wood
Farm

Wood
Farm

Gaddesden Row

N

Briden's Camp

0.5 miles

Gaddesden
Place

START

they mark the line of an otherwise hidden road, and the approach is fairly fast.

Cross the road (5 miles), and continue in the same direction up the track opposite. Climb gradually alongside the mature hedge that marks the edge of the field, to, at a levelling, a right turn. Follow this as it zig-zags towards the line of pylons, just before which it is brought up short by a holly bush (5.6 miles).

The direction we want is left, and this fortunately seems to carry less horse traffic, the riding therefore becomes rather easier. As Wood Farm away to the left is passed, the horizon takes on a more sharply defined aspect. This is what we want to see, as it can only mean one thing, downhill! So it is. The descent alongside a field has very good visibility, so if clear can be enjoyed to the full. That long uphill on the road now seems worthwhile!

After swooping down, the track climbs again briefly, before a final drop as it curves rightwards to the road. This is reached at 7.4 miles, and a left turn brings us again to the A 4146, where a right and a left take us back to the car park in less than a quarter of a mile.

Local bike Shops-   Hemel Hempstead Cycle Centre
57 High Street
Hemel Hempstead
Tel. (01442) 242410

Leisure Wheels
89 Old High Street
Hemel Hempstead
Tel. (01442) 213401

R & M Sports
30 Stoneycroft
Warners End
Tel. (01442) 258035

Places of Interest-   See Route 6 plus

St. Mary's in Hemel is
Hertfordshire's most complete
Norman Parish Church and
there is also pleasant parkland
alongside the River Gade.

Piccots End has important
medieval wall paintings housed
in a cottage, although these are
not currently open to the
public.

First Bridleway on Route 6

6. NOMANSLAND.

DISTANCE:	10 miles/16 km (4.5 miles/7.2 km on roads).
HEIGHT GAIN:	197 ft/60 m.
TIME:	2 to 2.5 hours.
MAP:	OS 1:50 000 Sht 166
CHILDREN:	Not Recomended - Very Busy Road.
WINTER:	Fairly Suitable.
START:	OS 171123

Common land is rather unusual in this area, and this route makes the most of the tracks and byways around Nomansland Common. It is a better summer route than winter, as parts of it can get very muddy with the passage of horses. It starts from the first car park on the unclassified road just off the B 651 (OS 171123). However if you are carrying your bicycle on the roof the barrier may prevent your entering. Fear not, there is another car park, albeit smaller, just down the road.

Leave either car park away from the B 651 and follow the delightful road across the common. After a mile turn right into Ferrers Lane at Ayres End Cottages, and at 1.2 miles take the bridleway on the left. This well surfaced way leads uphill through trees to become first an unsurfaced lane, then a gravel one as it emerges on to the road at the Three Horseshoes pub (2.1 miles).

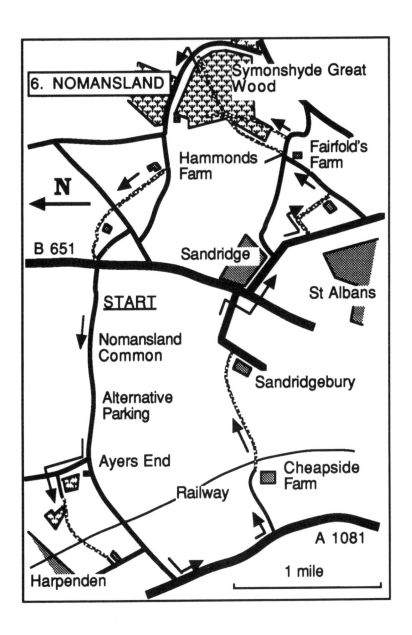

6. NOMANSLAND

Symonshyde Great Wood

Hammonds Farm

Fairfold's Farm

N

B 651

Sandridge

St Albans

START

Nomansland Common

Sandridgebury

Alternative Parking

Ayers End

Cheapside Farm

Railway

A 1081

Harpenden

1 mile

Turn left, and follow the road to the tee-junction and a right turn. This soon leads to the A 1081, and its attendant fast traffic (2.6 miles), where we turn towards St Albans. Although a busy road a narrow lane exists on the left for cycles, or on the other side is a cycle lane remote from the road. This purgatory only lasts for about three quarters of a mile until a tarmac surfaced bridleway carries us towards Cheapside Farm.

At the farm (3.9 miles) the bridleway makes an abrupt left turn to a gate. This is used to gain access to the field beyond which the route traces a diagonal line across to another gate. The field normally has grazing animals, so it is very important to shut the gates behind you.

At the second gate the track is squeezed down by a narrow railway bridge before emerging between trees and a wire fence on the other side. Typical of all restrained bridleways this can be very muddy in winter, a fact aggravated by the nearby presence of stables. In good conditions however it soon leads to the road at Sandridgebury (4.6 miles). In bad, abandon all hope of riding!

Once on the road it is all downhill to Sandridge, where, as the road emerges on to the B 651 a seat is provided expressly for the use of weary, muddied cyclists. Having covered 5 miles it always seems a pleasant place to stop for a drink. However if of sterner stuff just turn right into High Street, and almost immediately left at the Rose and Crown pub.

After a further half mile a motor cycling prohibited sign is the first indication of the next bridleway. This leads off towards Nashe's Farm, and climbs fairly steeply on a variable surface to a right angle turn where it levels out. At 5.8 miles the track becomes cinder covered, and soon emerges onto the road at 6.1 miles where a left turn is made onto the narrow lane.

Follow this pleasantly to the T-junction and turn right. Pass Fairfold's Farm, and just on the right hand bend turn left onto the bridleway alongside the field. This is not a right of way, but is permissive only, although the notice has every appearance of having spent many years in the weather (6.8 miles).

This is very narrow, and at first gravel surfaced, but it soon becomes potentially muddy as it climbs towards the second gate. Past the gate the way levels and enters the edge of the wood, at first running alongside fields on the right. Just inside the wood, the first of many obstacles is reached, where a small tree lies across the track. Bunny-hop (or fall off!) over this and continue to a path junction and a ditch.

The ditch runs parallel to the direction we must take, and the cycling now encountered is by far the best woodland riding to be found on any of the routes in this book. The wood closes in and has an almost wilderness feel to it, well it does until a wooden post is reached with two blue arrows on it!

Follow the right-hand direction, which leads via a broad track covered with the detritus of managed woodland. Branches and foliage lie in tangled masses across the route. Do not despair however for a well used path has appeared to the right, which picks its way through the trees. Do not however venture into the wood, as it is private property, and there are frequent signs regarding access.

Back on the main track there are often some huge,and deep, puddles to contend with before the final well surfaced rise to the road. This last stretch of dense woodland seems to be the home to many Jays which may regularly be seen as they screech their way from tree to tree, and soon brings us to the gate by the road.

7.7 miles, and a left turn on to the road is made. Road is actually too grand a word for this particular lane, which rises and falls, as it skirts the edge of Symonshyde Great Wood, and then narrowly down to Hammonds Farm (8.6 miles).

At the farm, a bridleway leads through the out-buildings, following, rather strangely, considering its status, what appear to be footpath signs. There is however, also a sign requesting no riding on the grass verges. Still, a bridleway it is, well surfaced at first, but soon deteriorating as it follows the edge of a field, to emerge rather dangerously onto a road. It descends a steep ramp through a gap in the hedge to arrive without warning. Take care!

Immediately opposite, the way continues, passing behind Nomansland Farm it bears slightly rightwards and soon reaches the pleasant grass of the common as well as the less pleasant B 651 (9.75 miles). All that is left is to follow the road back across Nomansland Common to your chosen car park.

Local bike shops - Bicycle Connection
117 Victoria Street
St. Albans
Tel. (01727) 843999

Harpenden Cycles
115 Southdown Road
Harpenden
Tel. (01582) 461963

Hot Wheels
22 Catherine Street
St. Albans
Tel. (01727) 842020

St. Albans Cycles
9 St. Brelades Place
Jersey Farm
Tel. (01727) 847477

Town and Country Bikes
18 Station Road
Harpenden
Tel. (01582) 767020

Townsends
169 Hatfield Road
St. Albans
Tel. (01727) 851208

Places of Interest -   The city of St Albans, named by
the Saxons after the first
English Martyr, has too
many attractions to list. Roman
ruins, a huge cathedral and
many other fine buildings make
this a place well worth a visit.

Kingsbury Water Mill in St
Michael's Village is an 18th
century mill on the River Ver. It
houses a small shop and serves
refreshments (Fresh Waffles).

7. OUGHTON HEAD LOOP

DISTANCE:	9.5 miles/15.2 km (2.8 miles /4.5 km on roads).
HEIGHT GAIN:	187 ft/57 m.
TIME:	1.5 to 2 hours.
MAP:	OS 1:50 000 Sht 166
CHILDREN:	Fairly Suitable.
WINTER:	Very Suitable.
START:	OS 201326

Even though of relatively modest length this interesting route contains a gratifying amount of rough riding. It starts from the Wilbury Hill picnic area (OS 201326), which boasts adequate parking, and passes several pubs, most of which have gardens. The highlight of the trip is however the ride to Oughton Head, where the stream springs from the earth bank.

Leave the car park in a rightwards direction, and almost immediately turn right onto the track leading downhill. Follow this, passing a couple of seats, towards the railway level crossing (1.1 miles). The gates of this make getting a cycle through impossible, and the actual crossing is footpath only, so under no circumstances may bikes be taken across. Be warned, trains pass this point at speeds of up to 100 mph!

So unless you wish to view the line, turn right at the bridleway junction by the seats and follow the track to the farm,

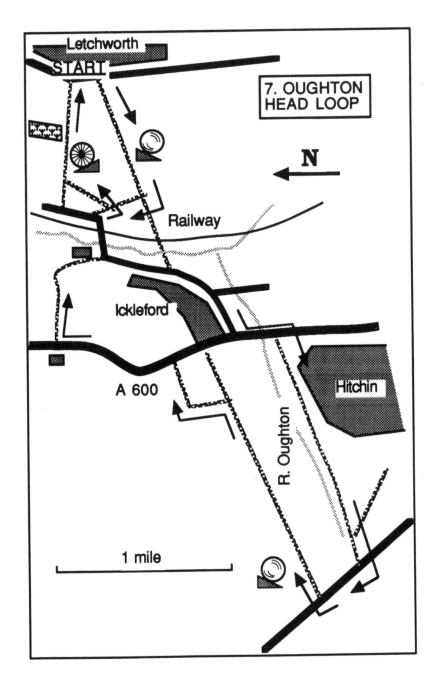

Letchworth

START

7. OUGHTON HEAD LOOP

N

Railway

Ickleford

A 600

R. Oughton

Hitchin

1 mile

where a continuation leads on to the road. Part of this is used on the return ride.

1.6 miles, and the road is reached just outside Ickleford. Turn left and pass under the railway, and continue through the village to the church. From here it is possible to go back up the Icknield Way to visit Jerry's Hole, a pond which is also a local conservation area, crossing a rickety wooden bridge on the way.

Back at the road continue along until at 2.5 miles Bedford Road is reached. Turn left, and after 0.2 miles at a bridge over the River Oughton, a bridleway carries the route delightfully alongside the stream. This gives about 1.5 miles of excellent and easy riding to Oughton Head, the source of the river, and at 4.3 miles emerges onto the road at a pumping station.

Turn briefly right, then right again onto the signed bridleway, this is shown as a 'white road', and designated as the Icknield Way on the 1:50 000 OS map. This drops down narrowly through bushes, and care should be exercised, as it is impossible to see what may be coming the other way. It however soon opens out into a broad grassy track, and easier going.

Passing the farm, continue to the bridleway leading off rightwards alongside a row of small trees. At the end of the trees turn right and follow the track outlining fields to the road, now visible by the conspicuous white houses (6.9 miles). Turn left here, and cycle along for 0.6 miles until the New Inn is reached.

If you can avoid turning into their car park, cross the road and take the well surfaced, at first at least, bridleway signposted to Lower Green. This has just about every surface imaginable, and winds, basically level to the road again just to the north of Ickleford (8.5 miles) on the Lower Green.

A left here soon brings the road round under the railway, and after a few yards the bridleway on the right descended earlier. Follow this through the farm, turning left past the barns. A generally good track then climbs gradually up the hill, before levelling out and giving easier riding alongside hedges to the road by the picnic area (10 miles). All that remains is to turn right along the grass verge (watch out for the drainage channel!) and drop down into the car park again.

Local Bike Shops-   See Route 4, plus

Letchworth Cycle Centre
20 The Wynd
Letchworth
Tel. (01462) 683615

Warboys Cycles
45 Leys Avenue
Letchworth
Tel. (01462) 685911

Places of Interest-   Standalone Farm Centre just outside Letchworth is an open farm of special interest to children.

8. CANAL SUMMIT AND ALDBURY

DISTANCE:	17.4 miles/27.8 km (6 miles/9.6 km on roads).
HEIGHT GAIN:	377 ft/115 m.
TIME:	3 to4 hours.
MAP:	OS 1:50 000 Sht 165
CHILDREN:	Fairly Suitable but Canalside Riding and Long.
WINTER:	Fairly Suitable.
START:	OS 919141

Note that is necessary to obtain a BWB canal cycling permit before attempting this route. See address in back of book.

Combining some of the best scenery in the area with some of the best bridleways, this long route has it all. Some fine villages are visited en route, and the church at Edlesborough, standing high on its mound is a delight. Incidentally should you be late finishing this route take heed. The ghost of Dick Turpin is said to ride the road beside the church at night.

From the British Waterways car park (note, small charge) at Marsworth (OS 919141) set off along the canal away from the village. The tow-path first rises to the bank of Marsworth Reservoir, used to maintain the level of the canal as this is the highest point, before dropping again to canal-side level. Soon the bridge and dry-dock at the Wendover Arm, then the works at

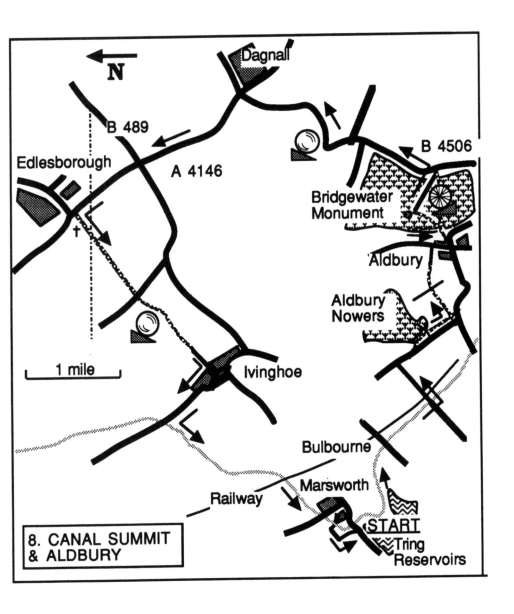

N

Dagnall

B 489

Edlesborough

A 4146

B 4506

Bridgewater
Monument

Aldbury

Aldbury
Nowers

1 mile

Ivinghoe

Bulbourne

Railway

Marsworth

8. CANAL SUMMIT
& ALDBURY

START
Tring
Reservoirs

Bulbourne are passed. Go under the road bridge, and continue to the high one carrying Marshcroft Lane over the canal (1.6 miles). Pedal steeply up, and turn left through Marshcroft Farm to Park Hill Farm, where there is a sign requesting cyclists to dismount. Walk down to the road and turn right.

At 2.3 miles a bridleway is reached leading between fences until emerging on a farm track. It is necessary to go slightly downhill here to continue the route along the lower edge of the trees. Muddy at first it soon improves to become a wide prepared track giving superb riding on a sandy surface.

Make the most of this, because in less than a mile a bridleway branches off steeply leftwards and through a gate. Relatively open at first the way is soon contained within fences and hedgerows, and with stables situated at the road end comes in for a lot of horse traffic. In wet weather this can be seriously muddy, and it is then probably better to take the road to Aldbury! In this case continue along the sandy track, and turn left onto Station Road.

Assuming the bridleway was braved, at 4 miles turn right onto the road, which soon leads to Aldbury village. One of the gems of this part of the Chilterns, Aldbury is blessed with pubs, a tea room and a village shop, as well as seats on the green, so you have a good choice of refreshments. The village is well worth looking round, with its old houses, pond and ancient stocks (last used it is said in 1898), a good excuse to play the tourist.

Fortified, and you'll need to be, leave the village by the Tom's Hill road to a bridleway between buildings to the left (4.3 miles). Signposted to Monument, Tea Rooms and Shop the going is excellent, just as well really, as it starts steep and grinds relentlessly up the hill. Fortunately the views over Aldbury and the surrounding countryside make any stops feel slightly less embarrassing.

At 4.9 miles the track comes out beside the monument to the Duke of Bridgewater, who was responsible for the building of the Grand Union Canal, and a rest may be taken in the tea rooms or shelter, and of course a visit to the column itself.

Ride along the surfaced track to the road and turn left, passing through Ringshall, and after a fast and winding downhill, to the crossroads at Dagnall. Left again, and in about 1.5 miles straight across the roundabouts to continue along the A 4146. Just by the church in Edlesborough a bridleway sign at a gate is found on the left (10.4 miles). This gives one of the best off-road rides in the area, 2.5 miles of continuous but varied cycling, with only one road crossing to break the rhythm before reaching Ivinghoe at 12.9 miles.

Turn right, then right again onto the B 488, perhaps taking a little time off to visit the 18th century Ford End watermill on the way, and continue to the canal bridge. Make a sharp turn downhill to the tow-path, and turn right (14.3 miles). All that remains is to cycle pleasantly alongside the canal (a good pub and a small thatched shop selling hot and cold drinks may be found at Marsworth) until at 16.9 miles the Grand Union Canal South Waterway Office is reached.

Here it is necessary to get the cycle up to road level before crossing the narrow bridge over the Aylesbury Arm. Follow the road down, leftwards round a bend, and out onto the B 489 at the foot of the reservoir. A brief burst up the road, and turn right into the car park.

Local Bike Shops-   See Route 15 plus

Dee's Cycles
317 High Street
Berkhampstead
Tel. (01442) 877477

Places of Interest-   Nearby Tring has an
interesting Natural History
museum.

If live and wild animals are
more your thing then the Tring
Reservoirs are famous for
waterfowl, and footpaths run
around them.

Berkhamsted has the sparse
remains of a Norman castle
where William of Normandy
received the surrender of the
Saxon noblemen. It was pulled
down in the mid 19th century
to make way for the new
railway!

9. THREE LOCKS

DISTANCE:	10 miles/16 km (4.2 miles/6.8 km on road).
HEIGHT GAIN:	196 ft/60 m.
TIME:	2.5 hours.
MAP:	OS 1:50 000 Sht 165
CHILDREN:	Very Suitable but Canalside Riding.
WINTER:	Very Suitable.
START:	OS891283

Note that is necessary to obtain a BWB canal cycling permit before attempting this route. See address in back of book.

Another route using canal towpaths, which although shorter than route 8, demands, for the water-side section, more attention as the banks are not so good. It has good parking at the start (OS 891283) and a convenient pub and picnic area, the former having a children's play area.

Leave the pub in a northerly direction, and cycle along the tow-path for 0.6 miles to the next bridge, which carries a large sign advertising the Dolphin pub in Stoke Hammond. Cross the bridge, and continue through the gates towards Paper Mill.

At 0.8 miles the River Ouzel is crossed by the buildings, and our bridleway goes straight ahead, well surfaced, but slightly uphill. Just past the farm the going gets a little muddier, which unfortunately coincides with a slight steepening. However the riding soon becomes easier, as the surface changes to compacted sand. After a gate, it steepens still more as it climbs towards the skyline and an area of gorse, with far-ranging views across the surrounding countryside.

Just as well for the legs, it soon goes down hill to reach the road at Partridge Hill (1.3 miles). By looking right the signpost showing the continuation of our route can be seen next to the road. This is again well surfaced, and leads narrowly down through tangled vegetation clinging to the high banks. As the sides open out a lake is visible in front, and the track skirts around this, bearing left to a set of signs.

It is important to note that these are private woods, and no cycling is allowed on any paths other than the Public Bridleway. Indeed horse riders have to pay for the privilege of using them, and there are actually signs barring bicycles from them. Please take heed.

The way rises pleasantly through the woodland and is generally fairly well-drained, except where some tree-felling has caused the surface to be damaged. This is the Greensand Ridge, which after a further short unsurfaced section comes out onto a drive by some cottages. At 2.4 miles a pair of ornate wrought iron gates lead out onto the road.

This gives excellent cycling through woods, passing the entrance to Stockgrove Country Park. Here there is a small picnic area and refreshments, along with toilets, but no off-road cycling, although it is worth taking a walk down to the lake to stretch a few different muscles. A short distance further, and the A 418 is reached (3.6 miles) and a turn made towards Heath and Reach.

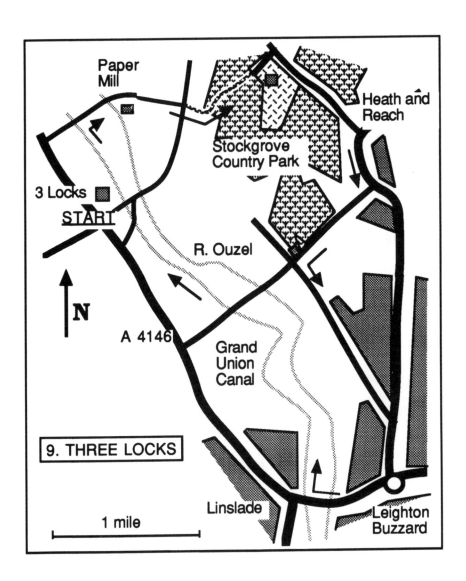

Paper Mill

Heath and Reach

Stockgrove Country Park

3 Locks
START

R. Ouzel

N

A 4146

Grand Union Canal

9. THREE LOCKS

Linslade

Leighton Buzzard

1 mile

Just on a left hand bend take the minor road on the right, and at the crossroads at Rushmere turn left (4.5 miles). This is then followed through increasing habitation to rejoin the A 418, which is followed into Leighton Buzzard.

At 6.4 miles turn carefully right and follow the road round, at first passing over the River Ouzel to the bridge across the canal. Drop down to the tow-path (6.8 miles), and breathe freely again. The remainder of the route now simply follows the canal, passing at first the pleasant waterside pub The Globe, then the small church at Old Linslade as it makes its way back towards Three Locks.

4.2 miles of excellent cycling later, the first sight, as you come round the bend, is of the canal falling away down the flight of locks. Quite a surprise, and one that can well be savoured over a drink!

Local Bike Shops-   See Route 15.

Places of Interest-   Nearby Woburn has something for everyone. There is the famous Abbey and wild animal park, as well as the well preserved town centre with its plentiful pubs and tea-rooms.

10. CHICKSANDS WOOD.

DISTANCE:	15.2 miles/24.3 km (5.2 miles/8.3 km on roads).
HEIGHT GAIN:	279 ft/85 m.
TIME:	3 to 4 hours.
MAP:	OS 1:50 000 Sht 153
CHILDREN:	Very Suitable - May be Split into Two Rides.
WINTER:	Very Suitable.
START:	OS 125404

Although using some tracks twice this ride makes the most of the area between the wooded hills surrounding Chicksands and the flat plain around Bedford. It is generally on good paths, and apart from one steep climb, flat. This combined with the fact that it could easily be modified into two shorter routes, each with little road mileage makes it very suitable for children.

Start from the Forestry Commission car park in Rowney Warren Wood (OS 125404) and turn left onto the road/bridleway leading to the former Chicksands base. Just before the base another bridleway leads off rightwards on the edge of the wood. Follow this pleasantly, just inside the wood, to a point where the track takes a sharp left hand turn to drop to the concrete road alongside.

Note. There is no formal access for bicycles to use any further tracks in Rowney Warren, other than the bridleway.

Turn right and follow this down to the road, noting the peculiar land mark on the hill. Not marked on the map! The road is reached at Appley Corner (1.4 miles), and a right turn is made. This takes us alongside a row of distinctly 'Des Res' and up to the tee-junction, where the sign to Haynes Northwood End shows the way. In Haynes village a tee-junction is reached (3.2 miles) by a bench on a small green.

Haynes 14th century church has in its possession the Cloth of Gold on which Queen Victoria knelt at her coronation. It is still used to decorate the altar during various festivals throughout the year. There are also a couple of shops and pubs in the village to meet the cyclist's more immediate needs.

Turn right at the junction, then almost immediately left into North Lane which boasts that off-road cyclist's favourite, a no through road sign. Follow this to the end, and just past the farm buildings take the sign-posted bridleway into open countryside again.

An excellent grassy surface carries us easily to a slight left around a field. Alongside a hedge it soon starts to descend towards the farms scattered in the plain below. Enjoy this, it is a good open downhill with plenty of visibility. Levelling out it passes sinuously across the now flat countryside and after a couple of gates onto a surfaced lane.

Follow this to the road (5.2 miles) and turn right opposite Cotton Cottage, and left onto the signposted bridleway. This runs arrow-straight towards Bedford, well surfaced, and with the Cardington airship sheds a prominent landmark to the right (as they are from all the routes in this area). At 6.2 miles, and immediately

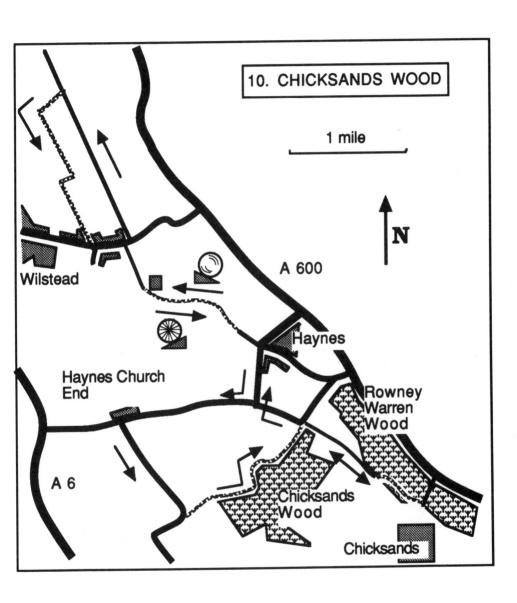

10. CHICKSANDS WOOD

1 mile

N

Wilstead

A 600

Haynes

Haynes Church
End

Rowney
Warren
Wood

A 6

Chicksands
Wood

Chicksands

opposite the sheds, a left turn brings us onto a narrower, but still good bridleway.

At the end of the field, turn sharp left, this runs parallel to the earlier path, and follow this through undergrowth to a widening. At a dog-leg the surface again improves, and a small brook is crossed for the track to run along the right hand side. The obvious track straight on is not a right of way!

At 7.5 miles a lane again brings the route onto the road. Turn left and cycle along to a large black barn, opposite which Elms Lane takes us past Manor Farm and a familiar bridleway. Familiar it may be, but I bet the gears will be different in this direction, as it climbs about 100 feet in just a quarter of a mile; until, puffing over, the road at Haynes is again reached at 10 miles.

You Are Never Too Young to Start

Turn right past the seat and follow the sign for Haynes Church End to a grass triangle and another right. Climb gradually through trees, with soon, a view across to Clarendon School, where a left turn signposted to Clophill is taken. This undulates and bends its way across the landscape, until at 12.5 miles, some white railings allow access to the best part of the ride. A bridleway stretches alongside Chicksands Wood as far as the eye can see. Solid beneath your wheels, the way curves to the left as it follows the edge of the wood.

At a small footbridge the Greensand Ridge Walk joins from the right, so the route is now marked by GRW posts topped with the deer symbol. Just on a sharp turn a little more pressure on the pedals is necessary as the track begins to climb slightly, then zig-zag as it levels out. At an obvious gap in the hedge an eroded, but nevertheless enticing little gully carries the way forward.

Easier to the right (but wet tree roots make the left hand side a little more interesting) it climbs out to another GRW sign. Easy riding around the edge of a field to a small wooden bridge and a way through to the edge of the wood again. Cresting a rise the first signs of civilisation for a while appear alongside the road, which is reached at 14 miles.

Over a final wooden bridge, turn right, and right again onto the concrete clad bridleway used earlier. This climbs gently to Rowney Warren Wood and the route back to the car park.

Local bike shops -

Barton Cycles
1 Church Street
Ampthill
Tel. (01525) 403133

Kempston Cycles
194 Bedford Road
Kempston
Tel. (01234) 851527

McKeever
Unit 17a, Kempston Mill Ind Est
Mill Lane
Kempston
Tel. (01234) 840316

Places of Interest -

Elstow village was most famously the birthplace of John Bunyan in 1628. There are also some attractive buildings including the 16th century Moot Hall.

Bedford is a pleasant riverside county town and has some interesting museums, an open air market and boating on the Longholme Lake just off the Embankment.

Ampthill is a fine old market town with the nearby parkland providing plenty of opportunities for walking, sorry no cycling!

11. ASTON HILL.

DISTANCE:	12 miles/19.2 km (6.6 miles/13.3 km on roads).
HEIGHT GAIN:	928 ft/ 283 m.
TIME:	1.5 to 2.5 hours.
MAP:	OS 1:50 000 Sht 165
CHILDREN:	Fairly Suitable in Summer - Can be Very Muddy in Winter! One Busy Road and Long Climbs.
WINTER:	Fairly Suitable.
START:	OS 891101

There has to be at least one ride in the area that everyone thinks of as the Chilterns. So here it is! Starting between Tring and Wendover, it traverses the area known as Wendover Woods and goes on to use the best of the bridleways in the area. It is also the only route in this book that cannot satisfactorily be cycled in the opposite direction as the track through Wendover Woods is one way only.

Just past the golf club on the minor road to St Leonards is the Aston Hill car park (OS 891101), this also gives access to a cycle dedicated forest track, information for which is posted on a board. Best to save this to burn up any surplus energy at the end! Our way starts easily with a descent of the road to the public track running through Wendover Woods.

Whilst coasting the few hundred yards or so to the start of the off road it is perhaps worth pondering on the days when Aston Hill was a stern test of early motor cars. It was a favourite place for a certain Mr. Martin to demonstrate the sporting prowess of his vehicles, giving rise to the famous marque of Aston Martin. Probably about the nearest any of us will get to a real one, although they have of course made mountain bikes!

At the barrier turn left onto the metalled track as it curves away from the road and passes the first of the car parks (pay and display). This climbs gradually for 0.7 miles before levelling out where another track joins from the left. The cycling is superb, through forest with far ranging views to Coombe Hill and the distinctive church at Ellesborough and across the sweep of the Vale of Aylesbury. Cars are allowed to use the track, but it is one-way, and they are limited to 20 mph.

Several viewpoints with benches are passed before the track becomes stony and the main car park with toilets and an information board is reached (1.4 miles). This also has a sign pointing to the Chiltern's highest point. Leaving this behind, the green exit signs are followed along the gravelly track, through a more wooded section, then across two ramps to the road (2.4 miles).

Turn right towards Chesham, and follow the road pleasantly to St Leonards. At a sharp left hand bend, with the small church just in front, take the narrow lane signposted to The Lee. Just on four miles, and at a sharp bend a bridleway leads into woodland at a pink cottage. Mainly on a well drained base, but with some sections liable to be muddy, this gives a good ride in just about any conditions to the surfaced track at Dundridge Manor (4.9 miles). A left here soon leads to another, and following the signs for Cholesbury, the tiny village of Buckland Common, a good place to stop.

By the green is a left turn signposted to Wiggington, this leads past the duck pond to the Tring road at 6.3 miles. Less than a

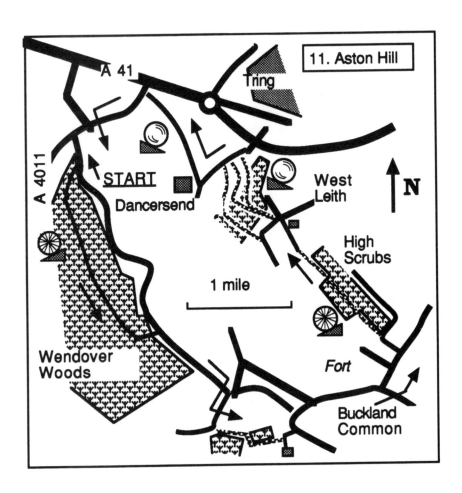

11. Aston Hill

A 41

Tring

A 4011

START
Dancersend

West
Leith

N

High
Scrubs

1 mile

Wendover
Woods

Fort

Buckland
Common

quarter of a mile down here, at a sharp bend a bridleway leads into the wood (shown as a BOAT on current maps) and this is followed for the next 1.4 miles to the road. The surface is very variable, good in some places, but can be very muddy in others, although with a little cunning it is possible to avoid the worst of the mud.

At the road there is a choice of ways, all of which lead steeply down the scarp on flinty tracks to emerge on the minor road just outside Tring. The choice is yours, although those to the west, nearer to Pavis Wood, link up with the rest of the route in a more satisfactory manner. At 8.9 miles it is necessary, whichever descent was chosen, to turn left onto the road.

Follow this gently up-hill to Dancersend Farm, and take the road on the right signposted to Aston Clinton. Easy, smooth riding gives a pleasant change to the previous descent, as the road drops steadily to join the A 4011 at 10.6 miles. Turn left and climb steadily along the surprisingly busy road as far as the signpost to Wendover Woods (11.4 miles). All that is left now is a stiff pull past the golf course and the entrance to the woods back to the start point.

Local bike shops -   See Route 8 plus

Mountain High
Tower Court
Horns Lane
Princes Risborough
Tel. (01844) 274260

David Boulton Cycles
Lloyds Bank Garden
Market Square
Princes Risborough
Tel. (01844) 345949

Wendover itself is worthy of some time, with just about every type of architecture imaginable represented, although Robert Louis Stevenson found it "a straggling, purposeless sort of place". The Cold-Harbour cottages were part of Katherine of Aragon's dowry and the Red Lion pub has seen such notables as Oliver Cromwell and Rupert Brooke pass through its doors.

Coombe Hill also moved R. L. S to words, when he walked these same hills in the late 19th century. A grand place, crowned by the South African War Monument.

For those with a more than a passing interest in traditional beer, the nearby Chiltern Brewery on the B 4009 may also be visited.

12. GREENSAND RIDGE

DISTANCE:	11.9 miles/19 km (4 miles/6.4 km on roads).
HEIGHT GAIN:	275 ft/84 m.
TIME:	2 to 3 hours.
MAP:	OS 1:50 000 Sht 153
CHILDREN:	Very Suitable.
WINTER:	Very Suitable.
START:	OS 112444

A route that has just about everything! Single track, firm surfaced bridleways, a climb to a superb viewpoint and attractive woodland. On top of all this, the road sections give quiet, pleasant cycling through some of the outstanding villages in the area. One even boasts a maypole!

It starts actually on the Greensand Ridge, Bedfordshire's main footpath, and there is limited parking just off the road at OS 112444, although care must be taken to not block any farm or field access. If parking here is not possible, the ride may just as easily be started from Cople village. Although the Greensand Ridge is a walk, a reasonable proportion is bridleway, including the section that now takes us away from the road.

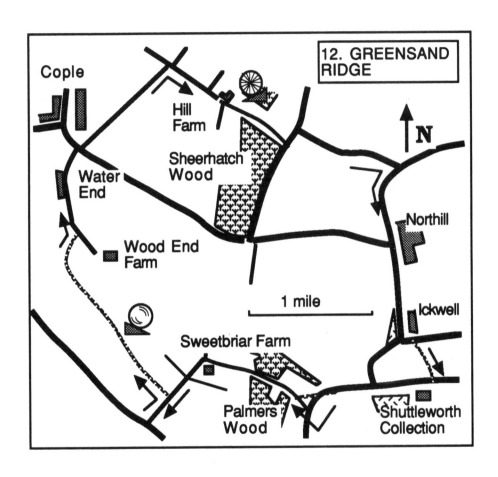

12. GREENSAND RIDGE

Cople

Hill Farm

Sheerhatch Wood

Water End

Wood End Farm

N

Northill

1 mile

Ickwell

Sweetbriar Farm

Palmers Wood

Shuttleworth Collection

Follow the good track for 0.3 miles, passing the small nature reserve on the left (entry on foot only please), to a crossing of ways and a signpost. Here turn left, noting the airship sheds at Cardington, to ride along the broad, grassy track. Just beyond a small knoll the way becomes narrower as it passes alongside a field to dive steeply leftwards through an alley of trees to an old fence.

This narrow single track continues until at 1.6 miles it opens out briefly to give views over farmland. They are only temporary though as we soon re-enter the tree lined tunnel and follow it past a right turn to the road (2.2 miles).

Left here, and pleasant cycling takes us down through the hamlet of Water End, where there are many thatched cottages, to the Northill Road at 2.7 miles. Straight in front is another bridleway. This gives easy riding on a good surface, following the line of a dyke, first on the left, then at 3.5 miles crossing to the right hand side.

About a further third of a mile of good track leads onto a small lane at a gas installation. Go right here, following it past the buildings (4.2 miles), to where it begins to climb towards the aerial on the ridge. Although fairly steep the climb is on a good surface of cinders, and just as it levels off, a seat beneath a tree is reached. This could not be better sited!

As the mast itself is passed the way becomes a normal grassy bridleway again as it passes around the wood, gently down hill to the road at 5.1 miles. Turn left here, and in a few yards right. Follow this to a tee-junction and then the sign for Northill. This village is soon reached, and at 7.7 miles Ickwell with its large green and maypole.

At a sharp bend in the road, follow the track round the rear of the cricket club until, where it turns left, a bridleway starts between high hedges on the right. Nearly half a mile of well drained track alongside a stream soon brings us out at the road just by the Shuttleworth Collection at Old Warden Aerodrome (8.4 miles). Apart from the aircraft and vehicle collection, the aerodrome also boasts a small café.

If historic transport is not your interest, stay on the road, and the next attraction is the Swiss Garden, just a short distance on. If neither of these take your fancy, then continue along the road to a large cream painted barn at 9.6 miles. This surfaced bridleway is the access road to Mount Pleasant Farm, and those beyond.

All is well, until just past Sweetbriar Farm the way becomes unsurfaced again as it enters a small wooded section. There are good chances of catching a glimpse of Muntjac deer (their silhouette provides the waymarking for the Greensand Ridge Walk) almost anywhere along this stretch, as the whole countryside seems to be alive with wildlife.

At 10.9 miles a GRW sign directs us leftwards across a wooden bridge, our old landmark of the airship sheds are straight in front now, and on to another sign. Follow this leftwards, still on good going, to a path junction at 11.3 miles and continue in the same direction.

11.6 miles into the route and the original crossing is reached where we turned off at the start of the ride. This gives an ideal opportunity for anyone for whom the route was not long enough to start their second lap, no need to even stop pedalling. Me, I'll just ride the further 0.3 miles back to the start!

Local Bike Shops-   See Route 13 plus

                         The Bike Shop
                         38 Shortmead Street
                         Biggleswade
                         Tel. (01767) 601001

                         Pedals
                         Church Street
                         Biggleswade
                         Tel. (01767) 313418

                         Sandy Cycles
                         15 Market Square
                         Sandy
                         Tel. (01767) 680548

                         Warboys Cycles
                         15a High Street
                         Henlow
                         Tel. (01462) 812927

Places of Interest-   The Shuttleworth Collection
                         at Old Warden Aerodrome
                         has a collection of vehicles
                         and vintage aircraft. Flying
                         days are held regularly in
                         summer.

13. OUSE VALLEY CIRCUIT

DISTANCE:	9 miles/14.4 km (2.4 miles/3.8 km on roads).
HEIGHT GAIN:	Negligible.
TIME:	1 to 1.5 hours.
MAP:	OS 1:50 000 Sht 153
CHILDREN:	Very Suitable but One Busy Road.
WINTER:	Very Suitable.
START:	OS 106499

This route is perfect for a winter's afternoon, or an evening ride from Bedford. It is relatively untouched by bad weather, as all the off-road distance is on well surfaced bridleways or disused railway line. It starts from opposite the dovecote in Willington village (OS 106499), but can be just as easily started from Priory Country Park in Bedford.

Assuming a start at Willington, ride down the good track for 0.3 miles, crossing a small stream where chub may often be observed in the clear water, to the cycle track along the disused railway line. This gives superb, flat cycling on a sound surface, at first twisting interestingly through trees to a crossing of a quarry road at 0.8 miles.

Take the continuation of the track slightly to the left, the bridleway leading off half-right is our return route, and ride easily to a gate. After the gate the going can be a little muddy, although nothing serious, as the limestone surface is breaking down due to a combination of use and natural weathering. Just after a second barrier the River Ouse is crossed for the first time (1.9 miles).

This is the start of the Priory Country Park, although the actual priory is long gone. It is believed that stones from it were used in the building of the dovecote and stables at Willington. Here a choice may be made between the tarmac drive or the loose surfaced track to the right alongside the New Cut. In 0.5 miles, by the Priory Marina pub and restaurant, a small bridge is crossed and a right turn made onto the road by the factory units.

Follow the signs for Cambridge, until at 3.2 miles, at Goldington Green, turn left, then almost immediately right. Follow the road across roundabouts to a signpost for Salph End and at a fork go right towards Renhold. At the Polehill Arms (5.2 miles) a bridleway leads away from the pub car park. Follow this easily for 1.2 miles to where it emerges onto the A 428. Turn right, and just before the MFI warehouse left onto a bridleway.

A concrete road leads past farm buildings to Willington Lock, where the river is again crossed. On the other side of the river the track becomes gravel, and soon leaves its bank with a right angled bend. At 7.2 miles a signposted bridleway leads off rightwards between fences to issue onto the aforementioned quarry track. At the time of writing, much work was being carried out here so extra care may be necessary on this section.

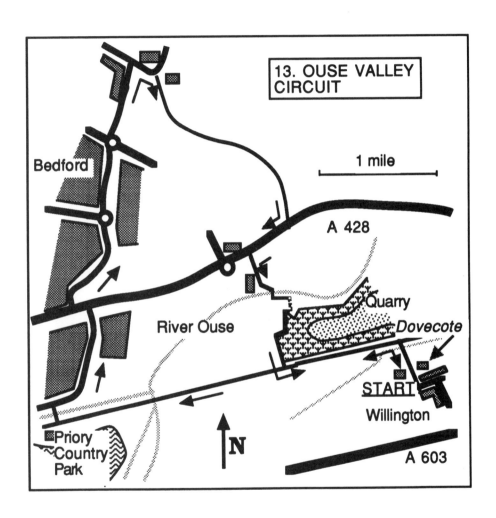

13. OUSE VALLEY CIRCUIT

Bedford

1 mile

A 428

Quarry

River Ouse

Dovecote

START

Willington

Priory Country Park

N

A 603

In half a mile the cycle track is again reached, and is this time followed leftwards, back through the gate and along the track to return to the dovecote and village of Willington.

Local Bike Shops-   Cycle King
                     40-42 Greyfriars
                     Bedford
                     Tel. (01234) 351525

                     Hawk Cycles Ltd
                     8 Greenhill Street
                     Bedford
                     Tel. (01234) 341932

                     Lawes Cycles
                     64 Tavistock Street
                     Bedford
                     Tel. (01234) 352257

                     M & N Cycles
                     34 London Road
                     Bedford
                     Tel. (01234) 344117

                     Michael's Cycles
                     54 Midland Road
                     Bedford
                     Tel. (01234) 352937

Places of Interest- See Routes 10 and 12.

14. CROMER MILL

DISTANCE:	10.4 miles/16.6 km
	(4.8 miles /7.7 km on
	roads).
HEIGHT GAIN:	164 ft/50 m.
TIME:	1.5 to 3 hours.
MAP:	OS 1:50 000 Sht 166
CHILDREN:	Fairly Suitable - But
	Wait For a Drought.
WINTER:	Not Recommended.
START:	OS 286310

It is said that everything has a good side and a bad side. So it is with this ride. In summer it gives an excellent trip, but after protracted wet weather it can, literally, be unridable. In dry conditions, the main bridleway gives a long, uninterrupted section of off-road, an impressive three and a half miles of basically flat cycling. It is returned to the start by quiet lanes, and a further short off-road section.

Some parking is available in a lay-by near the start of the bridleway opposite Broom Barn (OS 286310). From here the start of the route can be seen just on the bend in the road. Cycle easily, on a good surface to a gate at 0.2 miles; the track is marked as a BOAT on current OS maps. This carries the legend 'Track Shut To Vehicles Due To Poor Surface Condition', in winter it may as well read 'Don't Bother'.

From here the route is simple, follow the well worn track as it picks its way across the countryside, dropping to cross a small ford at 0.6 miles, where there are a couple of benches (too soon for a stop though!) while at 1.2 miles a BOAT is signposted off to the right. If you have been adventurous (mad) enough to attempt to ride it in winter this makes a good escape route back to the road. Mind you, the first bit is worse than the previous bridleway, but at least it is mercifully short.

Continuing along the Roman Road, the route drops to ford two more streams, the second can at times flood the track, and on to a gate where another way leads off to the left. Here the sides close in, and the track narrows (this section can be just about impossible following heavy rain) to climb gradually to more open countryside. Passing under some power cables the track becomes grassy, giving good cycling to the obvious buildings.

At the barn (3.2 miles) the way dog-legs through, past the buildings and onto the rough track leading to the road at 3.6 miles. Turn right and take the twisting, undulating lane to a T-junction, follow the sign for Nasty, and on the brow of a hill turn right, signposted Wood End (4.8 miles). This pleasant little lane gives superb cycling to the next section of off-road.

At 7.2 miles the road bends sharply right, and a No Through Road leads off the apex. Tarmac at first, then a good stony surface, it soon becomes a rutted, often muddy track just past an isolated cottage, where it bends round to the left. In dry weather however it gives good riding as it snakes across the countryside.

Ignoring all deviations to right or left, a bend is reached (8.4 miles) and the track rapidly improves. Cinders at first, then a firm stony surface it climbs gradually through high, bramble clad banks to emerge into Ardeley at a small housing estate. Follow it through the houses, past the village school, and onto the road at 8.9 miles.

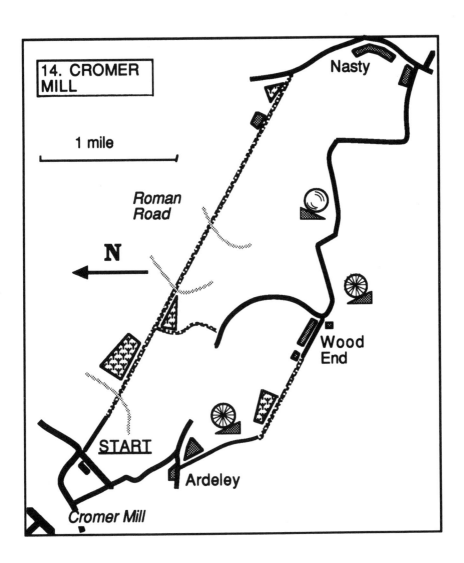

14. CROMER MILL

1 mile

Roman Road

N

Nasty

Wood End

START

Ardeley

Cromer Mill

Turn right, downhill to the pink painted 'Jolly Waggoner', and then left towards Cottered. The signs for Cottered will now take us back to the end of the first bridleway at Hare Street, or a narrow road can be used if a visit to the windmill is planned.

Local Bike Shops-   See Route 4

Places of Interest-   See Route 4 plus

Cromer Windmill is the last surviving postmill in Herts, and dates from 1720. Visits are possible on summer Sundays.

Nearby Baldock has a row of 17th century almshouses in the main street as well as a 15th century church with an interesting interior.

Knebworth House is a 16th century building, rebuilt into its present design in the early 19th century and has beautiful gardens.

15. WILLEN AND CALDECOTTE LAKES

DISTANCE:	12 miles/19.1km all on CycleTracks.
HEIGHT GAIN:	Minimal.
TIME:	1.5 to 2 hours.
MAP:	Milton Keynes Redway Guide available from Milton Keynes Borough Council. OS 1:50 000 Sht 152
CHILDREN:	Very Suitable.
WINTER:	Very Suitable.
START:	OS 873407

Not really comparable with any other routes in this book as the full 12 miles are ridden on Redways and their associated Leisure Routes, but although on the edge of a city it is still basically a rural route in character. The Redways, as mentioned before, are a network of paths for pedestrians and cyclists, where main roads are crossed by underpasses or footbridges. The other class of path used, the Leisure Routes (green dashed lines on the MKBC map) are designated as pedestrian priority, but cycles permitted, and tend to be more like park footpaths, so speeds need to be kept down a bit.

There is a Redway code of practice as recommended by MK Borough Council printed on the Redway Guide, which I urge every user to take notice of. Remember that people of all ages may be using the routes so it is especially important to ride with care and to be able to stop within your field of vision.

The Peace Pagoda is a conspicuous landmark on this eastern side of Milton Keynes, standing serenely on its mound beside Willen North Lake. At its foot on Brickhill Street (V10) is a large car park (OS 873407), and it is from here our route starts.

From the north end of the car park a path (Leisure Route) zig-zags steeply upwards to emerge alongside the Peace Pagoda in 0.4 miles. It then drops to the lakeside to join the southbound Redway. At the foot of the hill is a plaque describing the whys and wherefores of the building, and nearer the lake one informing what birds may be seen. However our way takes us alongside the lake and to the H5, where turning left, still on the Redway the road is skirted until a path leads down to the narrow neck between the two lakes. Crossing the slender channel near the road bridge, the River Ouzel is reached (1.1 miles), and a signpost for the Ouzel Valley.

In a further 0.7 miles the path drops to run alongside the river, following signs to Milton Keynes Village and Ouzel Valley, although where the way later branches off to the village we stay with the river. Soon a double gate is negotiated taking us into meadows alongside the river, where at 2.6 miles is found another plaque. It is definitely worth stopping to take a look, as the information about Great Woolstone Fish Ponds is imaginatively presented, showing an artist's impression of how the site may have looked in the 14th

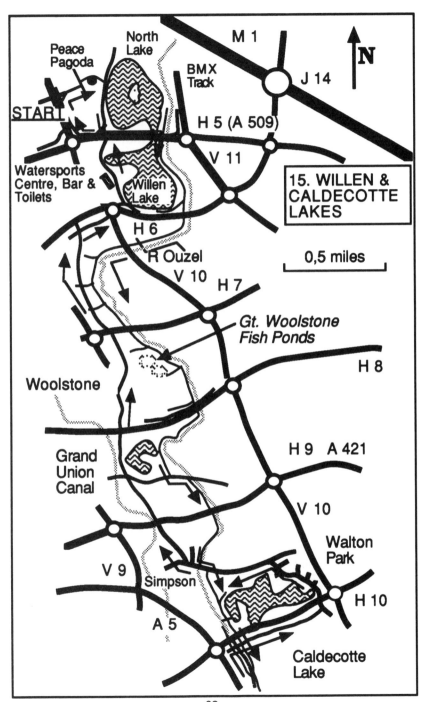

15. WILLEN &
CALDECOTTE
LAKES

century. The remark that for Fridays and Lent fresh fish was considered a status symbol, as those that could not afford it would have to eat salted fish, quite amused. One-upmanship is nothing new.

Ignoring any wooden bridges across the river carry on across several small cattle grids until a road is met on the outskirts of Simpson (4.8 miles), where the bridge is crossed to continue the path on the other side of the river. There is a signpost to Caldecotte Lake and a convenient picnic area at the junction of the path and the road, and as the route emerges from the trees a windmill is seen directly in front, although all is not as it appears!

Where the Ouzel slides over a small weir, drop down a ramp and through a small muddy section to climb again heading towards the road. The mill crowning the Caldecotte Arms pub is now on our left as we follow the South Lake Riverside Walk (5.8 miles) alongside Caldecotte Lake.

At 6.1 miles the river is crossed and the narrow winding path signposted Riverside Walk Simpson is taken northwards. Upon reaching Bletcham Way (H10), follow the Redway right alongside the road until another Redway, signpost The Waltons (7.2 miles) passes under the road to emerge in an estate of new houses. Soon a left turn is indicated to Simpson and Tinkers Bridge, and the brick bridge is again crossed.

Passing the church, a road to the right is taken, and just after a rise a Redway goes left signposted Woughton Park. Follow the canal until a crossing is reached at 8.8 miles where a right turn followed shortly by a left leads to Woughton and the route shares the village roads. As the road curves leftwards, just after some speed control ramps the Redway branches off to the right (9.8 miles).

Keep following the signposts to Willen Lake passing the Cross Keys and the Barge until at 10.6 miles turn right into Newport Road.

At Childs Way (H6) turn right, then under the road to Willen Lake, which is reached near a miniature railway, and the Watersports Centre. Ride northwards alongside the lake, the Peace Pagoda soon coming into view again near the H5 (11.5 miles). Follow the Redway left alongside the road to the V10, which is followed directly back to the start point.

Bike Shop   -   Chainey's Cycles
15 Benbow Court
Shenley Church End
Tel. (01908) 504004

Phil Corley Cycles
Unit 3, Stacey Bushes Auto Centre
Erica Road
Stacey Bushes
Tel. (01908) 311424

Grafton Cycle Co.
14 Stratford Road
Wolverton
Tel. (01908) 313290

Marina Cycles
Waterside
Peartree Bridge
Tel. (01908) 694313

P & D Cycles
35 Aylesbury Street
Bletchley
Tel. (01908) 642203

Roy Pink Cycles
127 High Street
Newport Pagnall
Tel. (01908) 210688

Trackers
59 High Street
Stony Stratford
Tel. (01908) 265200

Places of Interest - The Iron Trunk Aqueduct
carrying the Grand Union Canal
over the River Ouse just north
of Wolverton was first opened
in 1805, but collapsed in 1808
almost blocking the river. The
present structure dates from
1818, and has been in almost
constant use since.

Milton Keynes Centre is an
interesting example of modern
city planning with many open
spaces, and may be reached via
the Redway system.

16. BROMHAM RIDGE

DISTANCE:	9.5 miles/15.2 km (2.8 miles/4.5 km on roads).
HEIGHT GAIN:	131 ft/40 m.
TIME:	1.5 to 2.5 hours.
MAP:	OS 1:50 000 Sht 153
CHILDREN:	Fairly Suitable but Busy Roads.
WINTER:	Fairly Suitable - Some Clay Soils!
START:	OS 008503

Unfortunately this area does not live up to its promise. There are plenty of bridleways marked on the map, but on the ground it seems a different matter. Those that are really suitable for constructing a round route are all too often the victims of overzealous ploughing. The edge of a field may be OK on four long legs, but it makes for some tedious cycling. The route as detailed is still worth doing for the superb ride along the ridge that runs from Bromham to Bourne End, although the southern end seems to have fallen foul of the plough, so cannot really be recommended.

The best start point is Bromham, where there is a picnic area and adequate parking (OS 008503). Follow the road through the village towards Turvey. At a sharp right hand bend (0.3 miles) a bridleway, Thistley Lane, is signposted to Bourne End. This is followed on a good surface to a fork, go right, and follow the solid track to the gate leading down to the A 428 at 0.6 miles.

Cross the busy road, and climb the ramp opposite to the obvious bridleway sign and gate. This passes diagonally across a field to the corner of a wood, of which it follows the left hand edge. This soon takes a passage between bushes on one side, and the wood on the other, until at 1.4 miles a signpost is reached. This is the footpath to Stagsden, so is of course ignored.

We turn half left to ride between the field and the narrow line of trees. Where the trees temporarily allow, there are good views over the countryside to the left, while on the right is the small village of Stagsden. Very soon a minor road is reached by Astey Wood, and crossed to the continuation of the track.

This takes the form of a single track leading between the wood and a field. Beware of overhanging brambles! The wood soon ends, and we come out onto the open ridge, the slopes falling away to the valleys about 100 feet below. The cycling remains easy, and another road is reached at 2.4 miles.

This too is crossed, and the way recommences at a field. This has been ploughed out on the line indicated by the signpost, but a few yards down the road is a gap in the hedge, and a grassy thoroughfare stretching away towards the spinney. At an old post the way goes the other side of the hedge and beneath a tree 'arch'. As the ridge becomes broader, a line of posts mark the way towards the power cables, actually passing between the legs of one pylon until they begin to turn rightwards.

Continue following the stakes to an old gate post standing

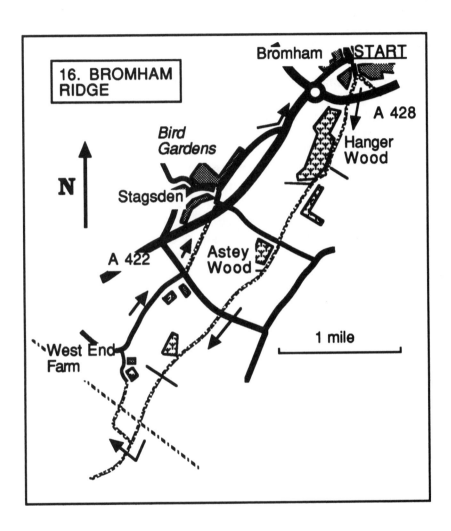

16. BROMHAM RIDGE

Bromham

START

A 428

Bird Gardens

Hanger Wood

N

Stagsden

A 422

Astey Wood

1 mile

West End Farm

99

proud of a base of large stones (4 miles). Turn right here and follow the field edge down and round to the left. The soil here is very heavy, so this section could prove troublesome in very wet weather. At another gate post the clay ends, and the riding is now on a good farm track, as it runs downhill alongside a small wood.

Cross a small bridge, and a final dog-leg brings us out onto a small lane at Haynes West End Farm and a right turn onto the tarmac. Just about totally devoid of traffic, this leads pleasantly to Firs Farm, where a fingerpost points down the next bridleway. This follows the line of a hedge at first, to a gap where it runs between fields. This is rather unusual as the one on the left is several feet higher than the field the track is in, almost like a breaking wave.

As the main road is reached the pulse quickens, all is not as bad as it seems though. Fortunately a concrete ramp takes the bridleway under the road, and up the other side into the village of Stagsden. There is a pleasant pub to the left, or the road by the church takes you to the Stagsden Bird Gardens, so there are adequate reasons for a rest! When the time comes, leave the village by the old Bedford road, which joins the maelstrom of the A 422 in about half a mile. Thankfully little time is spent on this, as at a roundabout we go straight across, and down into Bromham again to return to the car park.

Local Bike Shops-   See Routes 10 and 13

Places of Interest-   Bromham Mill is a restored
                       17th century watermill with
                       refreshments, open in the
                       summer.

17. WHADDON CHASE.

DISTANCE:	9.2 miles/14.7 km (2.2 miles/3.5 km on roads).
HEIGHT GAIN:	328 ft/100 m.
TIME:	1.5 to 2 hours.
MAP:	OS 1:50 000 Sht 152
CHILDREN:	Very Suitable Except Following Heavy Rain.
WINTER:	Fairly Suitable - One Section is Very Poorly Drained.
START:	OS 783338

It is difficult to believe the proximity of this route to the city of Milton Keynes, which is conveniently hidden beyond a ridge. From its start in the tiny village of Nash it takes in the best of the undulating countryside via a pleasing circuit of bridleways. Although there is over three hundred feet of ascent, it is generally in the form of short climbs punctuated with corresponding descents. This makes it especially suitable for children or road bikes.

An added advantage is the ability to start it from Milton Keynes itself, via Oakhill Wood which is served by both roads and Redways. It would even be possible to cycle from as far away as Newport Pagnell, with hardly any increase in the road mileage thanks to the Redways!

In Nash Wood End however, our chosen start is a small green, boasting a pump, seats and a duck pond, where it is normally possible to discreetly park at least one car (OS 783338). Crossing the stream leads to that countryside cyclist's friend, a no through road. Surfaced at first it soon becomes a somewhat muddy track once past the cottages. Even in winter this gives reasonable going as the foundation beneath the mud is quite hard, and it leads pleasantly through an avenue of bushes.

At a gate the bridleway is signposted diagonally leftwards and there are notices stating that riders must stick to the path that runs alongside the hedge. Please take heed! This rises slightly on a good grassy surface and gives far ranging views over the surrounding countryside before dropping to another gate.

The post wears the waymark discs of both the North Buckinghamshire Way, and the Mid Shires Way, and leads via a small bridge and a second gate to a rising track restrained by a rope fence (0.6 miles). This soon gives way to a more open field, where the route follows the obvious line of trees to pass to the left of Barnhill Farm.

Follow the farm access road until a faded and easily missed North Bucks Way disk on a telegraph pole points across a field to the right. Ride along the left side of a hedge to the small bridge, all the while keeping the church immediately in front. This bridge is best not approached at speed, as the boards will make short work of front wheels and tyres, and there is still a long way to go.

A good track has been left around the field edge, and it soon leads via a short, sharp ascent to Church Hill. Here the true right of way crosses to the right of the farm track, and enters the actual church yard at a gate. It seems rather incongruous cycling amongst the graves, so a little discretion and a short push could be the order of the day. It is only a very short distance to the next gate which leads out onto a more normal track at 2 miles.

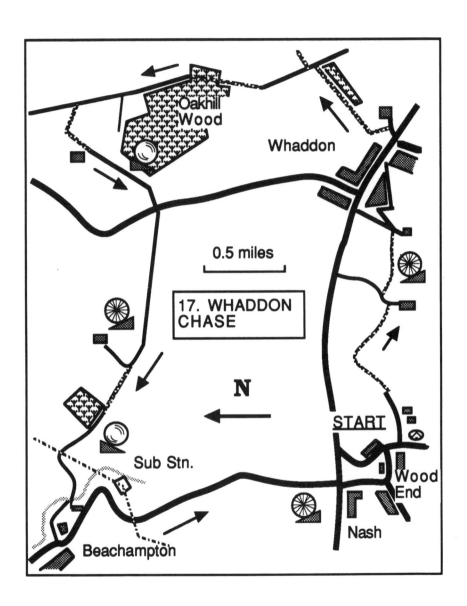

Oakhill Wood

Whaddon

0.5 miles

17. WHADDON CHASE

N

START

Sub Stn.

Wood End

Nash

Beachampton

103

Turn left and following the, by now, road, ride easily to the village of Whaddon. Follow the road in a south-easterly direction to where it bends sharply right, signpost Mursley, and continue straight on to turn into Briary View. Just down the road an old bridleway sign points through a gap in the houses and towards open country.

At a gate a further blue arrow points straight along a field edge towards the distant wood. This is soon reached and the field alongside, although not muddy is very badly drained, which may give problems in wet weather, and almost certainly will in winter. Fortunately the sloppy section is short lived, and a gate (2.8 miles) leads out onto the cinder-surfaced Swan's Way.

Turn left and follow, the now, easy cycling to a short section of grassy track which in turn leads to the perimeter of Oakhill Wood. Just a few yards into the wood is the end of one of Milton Keynes' Redways, and from here the going is on a pleasant solid track along the edge of the trees until after a slight climb a bridleway leads off to the left and yet another gate (4.4 miles).

Leaving the North Bucks Way behind, we now cycle alongside a hedge, hopefully keeping our wits about us. The next change of direction is easily missed, a gate in a gap in the hedge takes the route left again and down hill on grass to Shenley Dens Farm. Cycle around the green barn to join the concrete track which winds gently downhill to the road. Beware, the centre of the track is phenomenally slippery in the wet, but the concrete is just as hard!

At the road (5.4 miles) continue straight across on another concrete surfaced bridleway leading to Grove Farm. At 6.2 miles the track bends sharply right and a grass one leads straight across fields to Beachampton Grove. A few ups and downs are met by the wood, but the way becomes easier with the increasingly better surface, until after a pleasant downhill and the crossing of a ford, Beachampton is reached.

Immediately opposite is Grange Farm built in 1629, and one of the many interesting buildings in the village, making a short stop worthwhile. In one of them, the old Manor House, largely dismantled in the 17th century, Catherine Parr, sixth wife of Henry VIII is said to have lived.

Ford at Beachampton

At Main Street turn left, the return route is now all on road. Perhaps thankfully, as most of the height lost coming down from Beachampton Grove has to be regained. If all this activity has proven too much however, the weary cyclist could always stop at the B&B near Potash Farm. Mind you, is a mud-splattered mountain biker going to be welcome at an establishment offering "Executive Bed and Breakfast"? Perhaps best to just carry on!

After a final climb, Nash is reached and at the road junction the sign to Gt. Horwood is followed. A left hand bend, into Stratford Road, is followed by a right hander, just opposite the 'Old English Gentleman', and it is then but a few yards back to the green and a welcome seat.

Local bike shops -   See Route 15 plus

Seahawk Supplies
4 Castle Street
Buckingham
Tel. (01280) 817807

Places of Interest -   See Route 15 plus

Stowe School is a magnificent
mansion in Vanbrugh's finest style
with grounds laid out by
Capability Brown, and was the
former seat of the Duke of
Buckingham. A major National
Trust restoration of the gardens
and grounds is under way.

18. SANDY HEATH

DISTANCE:	8.8 miles/14 km (2.5 miles /4 km on roads).
HEIGHT GAIN:	164 ft/50 m.
TIME:	1 to 2 hours.
MAP:	OS 1:50 000 Sht 153
CHILDREN:	Very Suitable.
WINTER:	Fairly Suitable - Some Mud.
START:	OS 192484

Sandy Lodge is the headquarters of the RSPB, and is also the starting point for this ride, which stays just within the confines of Bedfordshire. Mostly on the light sandy soils of the area, and well surfaced bridleways, it makes for a pleasant ride, although some parts are still prone to mud. Apart fom the one descent, and corresponding climb it is basically flat, so making it particularly suitable for road bikes or children.

From the nature reserve car park, where there is a shop and toilets, just off the B 1042 (OS 192484) ride back out to the road. Immediately opposite, a well surfaced track takes you away from the traffic. Continue along the same track at a fork, and cycle pleasantly to the road at 0.6 miles, opposite Hasells Lodge, where a left turn is made.

In a further 0.3 miles turn right onto the cycle way to Sandy, and almost immediately right again through a gate. The bridleway so reached leads across fields on a good grassy surface;

this is our old favorite, The Greensand Ridge, and it descends through a couple of gates to Hasell Hedge (1.3 miles). Alongside the hedge the going can be a bit sticky, but at 2 miles a surfaced track is reached leading to Waterloo Farm, improving all the while as it runs down to the road at 2.6 miles.

Cross the road, and pass through the white gate onto an old tarmac path, which gives us a chance to spin the pedals a bit. After about a quarter of a mile the route passes between a tree and a waymark post to run alongside a ditch on a firm grass surface, and suddenly onto the perimeter track of a long disused airfield. The waymarking and quality of the paths combine to make this part of the ride a delight.

Simply follow the posts, as they direct the route firstly along the broken concrete, then at a small water tower (3.4 miles), onto a cinder track branching off rightwards. After a fork, where the left hand branch is followed (3.6 miles), this zig-zags around fields, with blue arrows at every corner. At 4.3 miles the surface becomes concrete as the way starts to climb towards the obvious house. Don't get too excited though, our way is not so easy!

Just at the white gate a bridleway arrow directs our route to the left. This is steep and well trodden by horses, in summer rough and bumpy, in winter....! This is either 'granny gear' or push, in winter it may be impossible to do either, so just get to the top which ever way seems best. Near the top however, the going does ease and the track becomes sandy before leading out onto a surfaced path (4.7 miles).

This gives way to grass, and is followed pleasantly to the road at 5.2 miles, where a right turn is made. A bit of speed on the road soon flings all the mud from the tyres and by the time the right turn towards Everton is reached the struggles are no more than a distant memory. At the next T-junction (6.1 miles) turn left, signposted to Potton, and at 6.6 miles right onto Mill Lane, which is also the bridleway to the Sandy Road.

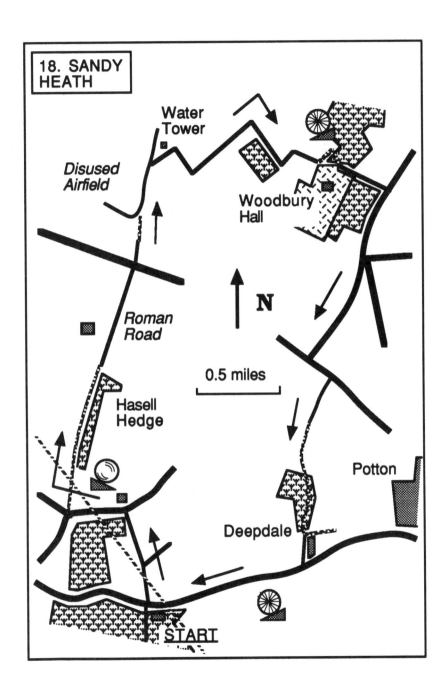

18. SANDY HEATH

Water Tower

Disused Airfield

Woodbury Hall

Roman Road

N

0.5 miles

Hasell Hedge

Potton

Deepdale

START

This is generally well surfaced, and heads towards the tall TV mast. At 7.1 miles the track enters a wood and winds through the trees on an unusually solid base, giving excellent riding until at a branching of the ways Deepdale is reached. Meandering through the tree-clad slopes, it is hard to imagine this is still Bedfordshire, the sandstone bluffs making it seem more like the Peak District, at least until the busy road is reached.

At 'The Locomotive' (7.7 miles) turn right onto the B 1042 and plod uphill for a mile to the entrance of the reserve, where a short spin of the pedals soon brings the route full circle.

Parking is free in the nature reserve car park, which is protected by CCTV. If not visiting the reserve itself, a couple of coins in the RSPB box would, I am sure, not go amiss.

Local Bike Shops-   See Routes 7 and 12

Places of Interest-   See Routes 7 and 12 plus

                     The RSPB reserve at Sandy is
                     106 acres given over to
                     British Wild Life. There are
                     several nature trails, gardens
                     and a shop.

19. QUAINTON HILL

DISTANCE:	15.6 miles/25 km (7.6 miles/12 km on roads).
HEIGHT GAIN:	580 ft/177 m.
TIME:	2.5 to 4 hours.
MAP:	OS 1:50 000 Sht 165
CHILDREN:	Fairly Suitable but Long with One Very Steep Climb.
WINTER:	Not Recommended.
START:	OS 804196

This is a relatively long route taking in as many bridleways as possible in the area, and linking them with generally quiet lanes. It passes through some attractive villages on the road sections, but the farmland which makes up some of the off-road component can be profoundly muddy after heavy rain, indeed some parts of it will almost certainly be unridable. It is also particularly important to close all of the numerous gates used, as in many cases an unfastened gate will allow stock to wander onto roads.

A small parking area can be found alongside the A413 just north of the Hardwick turn, where a footpath starts (OS 804196). Do not be tempted to use the footpath, but ride up the main road for

0.9 miles to a left turn signposted to North Marston. All gently uphill I'm afraid, but it does get the legs working. After a further 0.4 of a mile take the right turn down North Marston Lane where a superb twisting descent soon leads to the village. Ride past the green and follow the signpost to Hogshaw, a left turn.

A pleasant mile along the lane leads to the start of the first section of off-road which branches off rightwards at a sharp left bend (4.2 miles). Before zipping off down the track it is worth looking straight ahead where can be seen the mast on Quainton Hill; the return route goes over the top off the hill, so save some energy for later!

The bridleway starts as a pleasant short downhill on cinders, but at a gate the surface changes to a muddy, rutted track leading across the field to a double set of gates. Between the gates the surface is again good, but deteriorates again at the next field, which at the time of writing housed a small number of bullocks. Running alongside a small stream the way heads for another gate on the far side of the field where a welcome cinder track leads down to the road. This is the first mile of off-road, but is a good indication of what is to come. If this section is very muddy it may be worth reconsidering the remainder of the ride, as there is probably some pushing ahead.

Turn left on the road, until at 5.5 miles another North Bucks Way signpost points across a field. The bridleway here is also furnished with a stile, so it is probably best to lift your bikes over the fence rather than open the gate, as stock could get directly onto the road. Cross diagonally leftwards to another gate leading to a taped ride around the edge of the field, this contains the way to a six foot wide path very badly cut-up by horses' hooves. Soon however another gate leads into a grassy field and the way climbs fairly

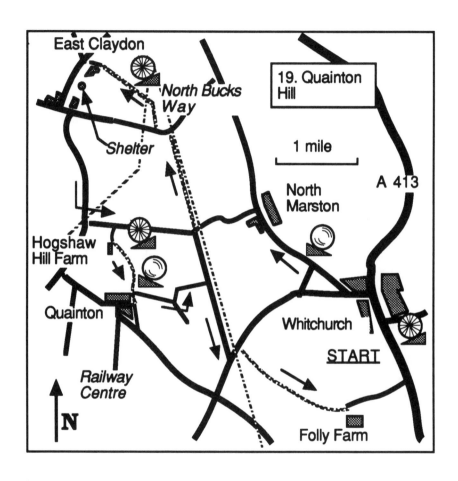

East Claydon

North Bucks Way

19. Quainton Hill

Shelter

1 mile

North Marston

A 413

Hogshaw Hill Farm

Quainton

Whitchurch

START

Railway Centre

N

Folly Farm

steeply to meet the surfaced farm track, which is taken until at 7.2 miles East Claydon is reached.

Turning left towards Botolph Claydon a thatched shelter is passed which gives an excellent place to stop, commanding as it does a good view over Quainton Hill. Ride through the village and follow the road round a right hand bend (8 miles) to the tee-junction and turn left. The road bears to the right towards Quainton and at 9.4 miles, on the left, a gated road is taken, running beneath the slopes of Quainton Hill.

A short distance along this road is a gate, where a bridleway leads up the farm track to Hogshaw Hill Farm, and access, via another gate to the steep flanks of Quainton Hill. The bridleway climbs steeply on grass up the rounded ridge, and will probably require a bit of pushing before the radio mast and underground reservoir are reached. At over 600 feet, the view from the top can soon make you forget those aching legs!

Fortunately what goes up usual goes down, and the run from the top of the hill is on a well defined track, still generally grassy, which passes through gates as it traverses the fields. Immediately in front are the sails of Quainton windmill, the tallest in Bucks at 65 feet and built around 1830. It is possible to visit the mill on Sundays between 10 and 1. A pleasant diversion.

Assuming the village is not to be visited, take the bridleway leftwards, signposted as the Swan's Way. After a few yards it curves rightwards again to a private cattle grid and the Ladymead Stud. To the left is a magnificent moated manor house, and we cycle alongside its boundary wall on the tarmac track until a path junction is reached.

Go left here and follow the continuing tarmac path uphill to the farm, where it turns right and contours the hill before dropping to a farmyard and the road. Turn right onto the narrow lane and continue to the larger road and a signpost to Pitchcott. A left turn and a few yards of road riding soon takes us to the final stretch of bridleway.

This starts innocently enough as a good cinder surface between a hedge and a fence, but after passing through a gate, the going can be very wet after rain. Follow the blue arrows on posts as the way leads through meadows to a straight path across crops, now the Aylesbury Ring. In winter this path is just about unpassable, the wet clay clinging to everything will soon render the bike unridable, and by now it will weigh about twice its original weight. I will probably make occasional trips on foot looking for abandoned bicycles half buried in the mud!

At a stream a gate leads into a field, where a continuation of the bridleway eventually passes to the left of the buildings of Folly Farm. A gate just alongside the farm leads onto the surfaced track which in its turn takes the now weary, or in winter, totally disillusioned, cyclist back to the A 413 and the start point.

Local Bike Shops-   Baker's
                     21 Buckingham Street
                     Aylesbury
                     Tel. (01296) 82077

Old Country Cycles
Unit D, Duck Farm Court
Station Way
Aylesbury
Tel. (01296) 398958

Places of Interest-   Waddesdon Manor, built by
Baron Ferdinand de Rothschild in
1874, and now owned by the
National Trust has a magnificent
collection of French art, and
very attractive gardens.

Bucks Railway Centre at Quainton
has a fine collection of engines and
rolling stock. They hold Steam Days
throughout summer when rides
may be taken on a short section
of standard guage track.

Aylesbury houses the Bucks
County Museum, and the St
Mary's Church has an
interesting tower.

20. ICKNIELD WAY.

DISTANCE:	23.6 miles/37.7 km (6.6 miles/10.6 km on roads).
HEIGHT GAIN:	810 ft/247 m.
TIME:	3 to 5 hours.
MAP:	OS 1:50 000 Sht 166
CHILDREN:	Fairly Suitable, but may be a bit long.
WINTER:	Fairly Suitable.
START:	OS 086259

This long route is really a linking together of routes 1, 2 and 7, and serves to show how bridleways that may not be suitable for a circular ride can be used. It makes for a good day ride, as there are plenty of pubs en route, many of them with gardens. The start point in Links Way (OS 086259) is the same as for route 1, although the recommended ride starts in the opposite direction. It also has the advantage that there are plenty of other possibilities for starting, and it could even be linked with route 3.

Leave the parking leftwards, and ride either along the golf club access road or the bridleway bounding the hedge. At 0.6 miles the club house is passed and a good track, the Icknield Way, curves rightwards dissecting the golf course. Before long the cinder covered way becomes stony, and climbs fairly steeply to a crossing of paths and a notice board about the Way.

Continue along the track, now partly paved with red bricks, gently downhill, and with wide ranging views, to the road (3 miles). Follow the same line along the road to the next section of 'off-road' starting at Treasures Grove car park, where there is another information board.

Route 2 leaves from here, so follow the first part of that, over the bridle gate and up the grassy track as far as the bridleway junction. At the monolithic sign a bridleway leads to the left. Well surfaced with grass, it runs between a dilapidated wooden fence and a newer wire one to a sharp S-bend before being funnelled in again. As it rises the views open out, those to the right hand side over Deacon Hill being most rewarding. Soon the slight climb is over, and it is all pleasantly downhill towards Pegsdon, and via a bridlegate, the B 655 (4 miles). Turn right, and the road, known locally as 'The Golden Mile', soon brings the next bridleway awheel.

If the road is golden, then the bridleway, reached at 4.5 miles, must be the jewel. It leaves the road at a row of wooden posts and runs alongside the edge of a hedge. Unusually for woodland edge tracks this is generally dry, and it soon reaches a deep coombe carved into the hillside on the left. From here it dives into a timeworn depression, turns half left and opens out to a broad grassy way with deep tracks of agricultural vehicles to contend with.

Running generally downhill, with tree roots and patches of slippery bare chalk to keep the cycling interesting, the village of Pirton soon comes into view. Entering an avenue of hedges the route,

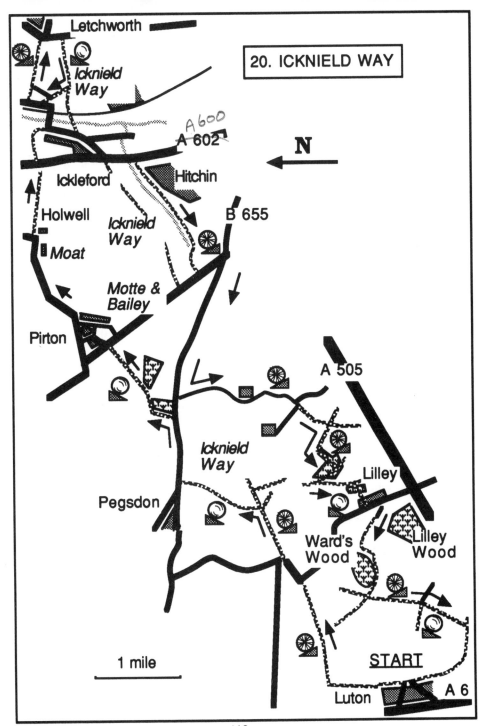

20. ICKNIELD WAY

Letchworth

Icknield
Way

A 600
A 602

Ickleford   Hitchin   B 655

Holwell   Icknield
            Way

Moat

            Motte &
            Bailey

Pirton

N

            Icknield
            Way

Pegsdon   A 505

                                           Lilley

                        Ward's   Lilley
                        Wood   Wood

1 mile

                                    START

                        Luton   A 6

still downhill, runs through a few shallow bends to reach a gate at the first buildings. This is open on the left, and soon after is an Icknield Way sign showing the walker's and rider's ways through the village.

It is a pleasant little village too, with several pubs, a green, an attractive church and even a castle mound, well worth stopping for a while. The temptations are certainly there! If not tempted, pass the Cat and Fiddle and the Motte and Bailey, ride past the church and turn right at the Fox to follow the signposted Icknield Way Rider's Route.

This takes us past the pond and village store, and then left into Royal Oak Lane, and on to a right turn at the signpost for Holwell (6.2 miles). The next mile or so on the road is easy, and after the moat and a left bend, an earth bank on the right hand side of the road signals the start of the next bit of off-road.

Starting between two small fields, this can sometimes be a little muddy at first, but it soon improves to become a fairly wide grassy track, with in places, a broken red brick surface. A line of stout posts mark the way across fields towards the distant road. a slippery wooden bridge is soon crossed, and the track narrows to follow a deep ditch on the left. The road is reached at 8 miles, at the New Inn, which has a garden and children's playground.

The continuation is a few yards to the right, down a fairly busy road, so care is needed here. Signposted to Lower Green, this is part of Route 7, and gives easy and generally dry cycling to emerge back onto a road at Ickleford Lower Green (8.4 miles). Turn left here and follow the road under the railway bridge and ride the short distance to the signposted bridleway on the right.

Follow this to the farm and turn left just past the barns, to climb gradually on a well drained track to a levelling alongside some hedges. This leads out easily onto the road by the Wilbury Hill picnic area. Turn right here, and then almost immediately right again onto the good track leading down hill to a bridleway junction and seat.

It is necessary to turn right here back to the farm, as there is no way to get a bicycle across the railway. At the farm, go straight through and via the track used earlier to the road. Flat cycling now leads through Ickleford (even more pubs and ice cream shops!) to the Bedford Road at 12.2 miles. Turn left, and in just under a quarter of a mile, right at the river.

Follow the bridleway upstream, passing Oughton Head, where the spring gushes from an earth bank to reach the road at 13.7 miles. This is a particularly pleasant stretch of cycling, and in summer the area around the river would make a very good lunch stop. Assuming you've avoided all the pubs of course!

At the road turn left and ride easily to the Hexton/Hitchin road and turn right. This is followed effortlessly to a gravel track leading to Wellbury House. It climbs fairly steeply to reach a cottage at 17.6 miles, and to its right a grassy track. This is good at first, but immediately after crossing the Little Offley road it can be very muddy for a short distance.

However the way soon improves, to run gently downhill to a crossing of ways. Turn right, uphill to the wood, which even in summer can be a little boggy. Watching out for fallen saplings ride and push though the trees on an easy to follow track and immediately upon exiting the wood head for the line of pylons to the right. Double back under the power lines and follow the track to the RUPP leading through a narrow wood (19.7 miles).

This gives a fairly steep descent to the road, and a left turn towards the church. Just by the church turn right and cycle up the narrow lane, past (perhaps) the Lilley Arms, or if your tastes run to ice cream, try the farm shop opposite the church first. Excellent!

At the end of the lane a narrow, sometimes very muddy track is followed. At Wards Wood the surface improves as it curls to the left, before becoming grassy again. At 20.8 miles a gravely track runs as straight as an arrow towards the prominent ridge. Climbing gently at first, it soon gets steeper as it nears the top where a good track leads along the ridge (see route 1).

Having panted our way up however, it is only fitting that we should be allowed a descent, and what a descent! Steep and winding on a good gravel surface, it is necessary to keep your wits about you as there are several places where it is not possible to see if anyone else is on the path. **No** points awarded for collecting a walker or horse rider.

Finally, at the foot of the hill turn right onto the broad track, ride past the new housing estate, and in about a mile back to the start, fit and ready to start another lap.

Local bike shops -   See routes 1, 2 and 7

Places of Interest -   See routes 1, 2 and 7

USEFUL ADDRESSES.

BEDFORDSHIRE COUNTY COUNCIL,
DIRECTOR OF LEISURE SERVICES,
COUNTY HALL,
BEDFORD
MK42 9AP

BRITISH WATERWAYS,
WATERWAY MANAGER,
MARSWORTH JUNCTION,
WATERY LANE,
MARSWORTH, TRING
HP23 4LZ

BUCKINGHAMSHIRE COUNTY COUNCIL,
COUNTY ENGINEERS DEPARTMENT,
COUNTY HALL,
AYLESBURY
HP20 1UY

BYWAYS AND BRIDLEWAYS TRUST,
9 QUEEN ANNE'S GATE,
LONDON
SW1H 9BH

THE CHILTERN SOCIETY,
P.O. BOX 1029,
MARLOW
SL7 2HZ

THE COUNTRYSIDE COMMISION,
ORTONA HOUSE,
110 HILLS ROAD,
CAMBRIDGE
CB2 1LQ

CYCLING CAMPAIGN FOR BEDFORDSHIRE
HAZEL MITCHELL
51 FALCON AVENUE
BEDFORD
MK41 7DY

CYCLISTS' TOURING CLUB,
69 MEADROW,
GODALMING
GU7 3HS

FORESTRY COMMISSION,
FOREST DISTRICT OFFICE,
UPPER ICKNIELD WAY,
ASTON CLINTON,
AYLESBURY
HP22 5NF

ICKNIELD WAY ASSOCIATION,
19 BOUNDARY ROAD,
BISHOPS STORTFORD
CM23 5LE

MILTON KEYNES BOROUGH COUNCIL,
SAXON COURT,
502 AVEBURY BOULEVARD,
CENTRAL MILTON KEYNES
MK9 3HS

NATIONAL TRUST, THAMES AND CHILTERNS REGIONAL OFFICE,
HUGHENDEN MANOR,
HIGH WYCOMBE
HP14 4LA

TOURIST INFORMATION CENTRES

AYLESBURY
COUNTY HALL,
WALTON STREET.
(01296) 382308

BEDFORD
10 St PAUL'S SQUARE.
(01234) 215226

DUNSTABLE
LIBRARY,
VERNON PLACE.
(01582) 471012

HITCHIN
LIBRARY,
PAYNES PARK
(01462) 450133

LUTON
65-67 BUTE STREET.
(01582) 401579

MILTON KEYNES
CITY SQUARE,
536 SILBURY BOULEVARD.
(01908) 232525

WILLEN LAKE WATERSPORTS CENTRE (CYCLE HIRE),
BRICKHILL STREET,
MILTON KEYNES
MK15 0DS
(01908) 670197

YHA NATIONAL OFFICE,
TREVELYAN HOUSE,
8 St. STEPHEN'S HILL,
St. ALBANS
AL1 2DY

Books Published by THE BOOK CASTLE

JOURNEYS INTO HERTFORDSHIRE: Anthony Mackay.
Foreword by The Marquess of Salisbury, Hatfield House. Nearly 200 superbly detailed ink drawings depict the towns, buildings and landscape of this still predominantly rural county.

JOURNEYS INTO BEDFORDSHIRE: Anthony Mackay.
Foreword by The Marquess of Tavistock, Woburn Abbey.
A lavish book of over 150 evocative ink drawings.

**COUNTRYSIDE CYCLING IN BEDFORDSHIRE,
BUCKINGHAMSHIRE AND HERTFORDSHIRE**: Mick Payne.
Twenty rides on and off-road for all the family.

**LEAFING THROUGH LITERATURE: Writers' Lives in Hertfordshire
and Bedfordshire**: David Carroll.
Illustrated short biographies of many famous authors and their connections with these counties.

THROUGH VISITORS' EYES: A Bedfordshire Anthology:
edited by Simon Houfe.
Impressions of the county by famous visitors over the last four centuries, thematically arranged and illustrated with line drawings.

**THE HILL OF THE MARTYR: An Architectural History of
St. Albans Abbey**: Eileen Roberts.
Scholarly and readable chronological narrative history of Hertfordshire and Bedfordshire's famous cathedral. Fully illustrated with photographs and plans.

LOCAL WALKS: South Bedfordshire and North Chilterns:
Vaughan Basham. Twenty-seven thematic circular walks.

LOCAL WALKS: North and Mid-Bedfordshire:
Vaughan Basham. Twenty-five thematic circular walks.

**CHILTERN WALKS: Hertfordshire, Bedfordshire and
North Buckinghamshire**: Nick Moon.
Part of the trilogy of circular walks, in association with the Chiltern Society. Each volume contains thirty circular walks.

CHILTERN WALKS: Buckinghamshire: Nick Moon.

CHILTERN WALKS: Oxfordshire and West Buckinghamshire:
Nick Moon.

**OXFORDSHIRE WALKS: Oxford, the Cotswolds and the
Cherwell Valley**: Nick Moon.
One of two volumes planned to complement Chiltern Walks: Oxfordshire and complete coverage of the county, in association with the Oxford Fieldpaths Society. Thirty circular walks in each.

**OXFORDSHIRE WALKS: Oxford, the Downs and the
Thames Valley**: Nick Moon.

FOLK: Characters and Events in the History of Bedfordshire and Northamptonshire: Vivienne Evans.
Anthology about people of yesteryear – arranged alphabetically by village or town.

LEGACIES: Tales and Legends of Luton and the North Chilterns: Vic Lea. Twenty-five mysteries and stories based on fact, including Luton Town Football Club. Many photographs.

ECHOES: Tales And Legends of Bedfordshire and Hertfordshire: Vic Lea. Thirty, compulsively retold historical incidents.

ECCENTRICS and VILLAINS, HAUNTINGS and HEROES.
Tales from Four Shires: Northants., Beds., Bucks. and Herts.:
John Houghton.
True incidents and curious events covering one thousand years.

THE RAILWAY AGE IN BEDFORDSHIRE: Fred Cockman.
Classic, illustrated account of early railway history.

JOHN BUNYAN: HIS LIFE AND TIMES: Vivienne Evans.
Foreword by the Bishop of Bedford. Preface by Terry Waite. Bedfordshire's most famous son set in his seventeenth century context.

SWANS IN MY KITCHEN: The Story of a Swan Sanctuary: Lis Dorer.
Foreword by Dr Philip Burton. Updated edition. Tales of her dedication to the survival of these beautiful birds through her sanctuary near Hemel Hempstead.

WHIPSNADE WILD ANIMAL PARK: 'MY AFRICA': Lucy Pendar.
Foreword by Andrew Forbes. Introduction by Gerald Durrell.
Inside story of sixty years of the Park's animals and people – full of anecdotes, photographs and drawings.

FARM OF MY CHILDHOOD, 1925–1947: Mary Roberts.
An almost vanished lifestyle on a remote farm near Flitwick.

DUNSTABLE WITH THE PRIORY, 1100–1550: Vivienne Evans.
Dramatic growth of Henry I's important new town around a major crossroads.

DUNSTABLE DECADE: THE EIGHTIES: – A Collection of Photographs: Pat Lovering.
A souvenir book of nearly 300 pictures of people and events in the 1980s.

DUNSTABLE IN DETAIL: Nigel Benson.
A hundred of the town's buildings and features, plus town trail map.

OLD DUNSTABLE: Bill Twaddle.
A new edition of this collection of early photographs.

BOURNE AND BRED: A Dunstable Boyhood Between the Wars:
Colin Bourne. An elegantly written, well-illustrated book capturing the spirit of the town over fifty years ago.

ROYAL HOUGHTON: Pat Lovering.
Illustrated history of Houghton Regis from the earliest times to the present.

BEDFORDSHIRE'S YESTERYEARS Vol. 1: The Family, Childhood and Schooldays: Brenda Fraser-Newstead.
Unusual early 20th century reminiscences, with private photographs.

BEDFORDSHIRE'S YESTERYEARS Vol 2: The Rural Scene: Brenda Fraser-Newstead.
Vivid first-hand accounts of country life two or three generations ago.

THE CHANGING FACE OF LUTON: An Illustrated History: Stephen Bunker, Robin Holgate and Marian Nichols.
Luton's development from earliest times to the present busy industrial town. Illustrated in colour and monochrome. The three authors from Luton Museum are all experts in local history, archaeology, crafts and social history.

THE MEN WHO WORE STRAW HELMETS: Policing Luton, 1840–1974: Tom Madigan.
Meticulously chronicled history; dozens of rare photographs; author served Luton Police for nearly fifty years.

BETWEEN THE HILLS: The Story of Lilley, a Chiltern Village: Roy Pinnock.
A priceless piece of our heritage – the rural beauty remains but the customs and way of life described here have largely disappeared.

EVA'S STORY: Chesham Since the Turn of the Century: Eva Rance.
The ever-changing twentieth-century, especially the early years at her parents' general stores, Tebby's, in the High Street.

THE TALL HITCHIN SERGEANT: A Victorian Crime Novel based on fact: Edgar Newman. Mixes real police officers and authentic background with an exciting storyline.

Specially for Children

VILLA BELOW THE KNOLLS: A Story of Roman Britain: Michael Dundrow. An exciting adventure for young John in Totternhoe and Dunstable two thousand years ago.

ADVENTURE ON THE KNOLLS: A Story of Iron Age Britain: Michael Dundrow. Excitement on Totternhoe Knolls as ten-year-old John finds himself back in those dangerous times, confronting Julius Caesar and his army.

THE RAVENS: One Boy Against the Might of Rome: James Dyer. On the Barton Hills and in the south-each of England as the men of the great fort of Ravensburgh (near Hexton) confront the invaders.

Further titles are in preparation.
All the above are available via any bookshop, or from the publisher and bookseller
THE BOOK CASTLE
12 Church Street, Dunstable, Bedfordshire, LU5 4RU
Tel: (0582) 605670